The Cell Chef Cookbook

Collection of Recipes by Tanner George Cummings

Freebird Publishers
www.FreebirdPublishers.com

Freebird Publishers

Box 541, North Dighton, MA 02764

Info@FreebirdPublishers.com

www.FreebirdPublishers.com

Copyright © 2016 by Freebird Publishers

This cookbook is a product of contributed recipes and recipes first seen in *The Echo*, a criminal justice publication produced by TDCJ staff for their offenders use. *The Echo* granted permission for the reproduction of non-copyrighted materials, provided credit is given to the contributors.

All rights reserved. No part of this book may be reproduced in any form or by any means without the prior written consent of the Publisher, except in brief quotes used in reviews.

All Freebird Publishers titles, imprints and distributed lines are available at special quantity discounts for bulk purchases for sales promotions, premiums, fund-raising, educational or institutional use.

ISBN: 1530091446

ISBN-13: 978-1530091447

Printed in the United States of America

Disclaimer
The publisher sincerely apologizes for any errors and/or omissions.

Freebird Publishers

www.FreebirdPublishers

Editor / Publisher	Freebird Publishers
Complied by	Tanner George Cummings
Production Services	AGO PER Karma Designs
Cover Designs	Cyber Hut Designs
Wholesale	Diane@FreebirdPublishers.com
Authorized Distributors	Freebird Publishers.com
(orders by mail, email, phone and online)	Amazon
	Barnes & Noble

Acknowledgements

Freebird Publishers would like to acknowledge and gratefully thank all of our contributors. Without their generosity this cookbook would not have been published.

The author would first like to thank Freebird Publishers for taking on the project of his cookbook and turning it into a masterpiece. To the wizard of an editor, Joanne for her (keen) magical eyes and superb comprehension of his writing. Not to mention her many splendid ideas and suggestions. For her countless time spent in preparing these many pages into an easy and enjoyable cookbook to read. Thank you.

Least but not last, to the many readers for purchasing this cookbook. In hope you relish the foods, drinks and desserts, as much as he did in trying every recipe and writing the details onto paper.

Additional Information

Annual subscriptions to *The Echo* can be purchased for $12. Money orders or personal checks must be made out to The Echo / WSD.

Correspondence via U.S. Mail must be addressed to, The Echo, P.O. Box 40, Huntsville, Texas 77342-0040. TDCJ offenders can write The Echo by truck mail.

The Echo has been in publication since 1928.

Dedication

The author would like to dedicate this cookbook to an unconditional friend who taught him how to make the best of what you do have. Billie Collins, you have given him unspeakable inspiration. Thank you.

In Appreciation

Freebird Publishers would like to extend a special thanks to Tanner George Cummings for his long hours, hard work and great expense in researching the recipes which made this cookbook possible. Tanner has gone to great lengths to insure, to the readers of this cookbook, that each recipe is complete, accurate and delish.

Table of Contents

Meals and Snacks	14 - 85
Sauces, Sandwich Spreads, Salsa and Dips	86 - 98
Drinks	99 - 118
Sweet Desserts	119 - 164
Glossary	165 - 170
Equivalent Package Sizes	170
Heating Sources	170
Index	171 - 179

Meals and Snacks

Columbian Rice	14
Spicy Mackerel Rice	15
Alguyen's Fried Rice	16
Dirty Rice	17
Cruz'n Rice	18
Cheap Chicken	19
Chicken Noodle Tortilla Soup	20
Orange Chicken	21
Lindsey's Ritzy Pate	22
Refried Beanie Chicken Winnies	23
Chicken Salad	24
Straight Strutten Chicken	25
Sweet N Sour Chicken	26
Todd's Tasty Tacos	27
Jalapeno Beef Tacos	28
Mystery Meat Tacos	29
Tacos ala TDCJ	30
Breakfast Tacos	31
Chicken Tacos	32
Fantastic Fish Tacos	33
Tippy's Spicy Tuna Wraps	34
Tamales	35
Cheesy Chicken Burritos	36
Chipotle Chicken-n-Ranch Burritos	37
Spicy Chicken Burrito	38
Mexican Pizza	39

Chili Pizza	40
Poor Mans' Pizza	41
Tuna Pizza	42
Jack Mack Pizza	43
Spam Pizza	44
Sardine Pizza	45
Chili-Beef Tips Pizza	46
Mexican Beef Crumble Pizza	47
Killer Frito Pie	48
Frito Pie	49
Chicken Chili Nachos	50
Sharp Cheddar Chicken Nachos	51
Chili Cheese Nachos	52
Jalapeno Cheese Nachos	53
Beef-n-Cheese Nachos	54
Simple Sardines	55
Sardine Spread	56
Slightly Sweet Nuttier Chicken	57
Poor Man's Spread	58
Sweet and Sour Noodles	59
Sweet and Sour Bowl	60
Lemon Fish Flips	61
Wicked Popcorn Soup	62
No Meat Spread	63
Hot Buttered Soup	64
Simply Scrumptious Ham Mac-n-Cheese	65
Commix	66

Tasty Spuds	67
Potato Salad	68
Potato Cake	69
Jeff's Spaghetti Daze	70
Prisagna (Prison Lasagna)	71
Stuffed Jalapenos	72
Diana's Stuffed Pickles	73
Becca's Faux Chow Chow	74
Tuna Noodle Salad	75
Mock Spam Subway	76
Beef Sloppy Joe	77
Ted's Po`boy BBQ Crunch	78
Tuna No Soup	79
Sweet N Sour Summer Sausage	80
Bentley's Deviled Eggs	81
Spameggish Sandwich	82
Breakfast Bowl	83
Chili Layer	84

Sauces, Sandwich Spreads, Salsa & Dips

Esco's Spread Sauce	86
Paul's Pizza Sauce	87
Special Sauce	88
Ala Sauce	89
Homemade Sandwich Spread	90
Dirty's Hot Salsa	91
Homemade Salsa	92
Lori Kay's Holiday Onion Dip	93

Beef-not- Chor-Chip Dip	94
Brent's Queso Loco Dip	95
Summer Sausage Chip Dip	96
Mistie & Lacey Dip	97

Drinks

Pretty Drink	99
Sweet Orange Mint Tea	100
Caffeine Late	101
Caffeine-Cino Rush	102
Allergy Sootherment	103
Homemade Chocolate Cappuccino	104
Orange Milky Mint Tea	105
Chocolate Milk	106
Simply Chocolate Milk	107
Peppermint Chocolate Milk	108
Green Hulk Cold Milk	109
Mississippi Mudslide	110
Remember Bennigans?	111
Butterscotch Cream Coffee	112
Margaret's Non-Alcoholic Strawberry Margaritas	113
Vanillocolate Coffee	114
Health Drink	115
Sweet Vanilla Sin Coffee	116
Chocolatey Rich	117

Sweet Desserts

Banana Nut Cheesecake	119
Strawberry Cheesecake	120
Ice Cream Cheesecake	121
Liv's Lemon Cheesecake	122
Liv's Apple Cinnamon Cheesecake	123
Liv's Strawberry Ice cream Cheesecake	124
Liv's Chocolate Cheesecake	125
Loving Lemon Meringue Pie	126
Wild Bill's Cream cheese Spread	127
Fruddy's Banana Pudding	128
Margaret's Creole Banana Pudding	129
Cherry's Banana Pudding	130
Diana's Banana Pudding	131
J.C.'s Lemon Pudding	132
Granola Bars	133
Sweet Granola Pie	134
Charlie's Butterscotch Brownies	135
Mock Brownies	136
Mud Pie Brownies	137
Rich Peanut butter Brownies	138
Fudge Cookie Sandwiches w/ Butterscotch Icing	139
Peanut butter Fudge Bar w/ Peppermint Icing	140
Nutty Chocolate w/ Peanut Butter Icing	141
Chocolaty Peanut butter Bars	142

Chocolate Vanilla Wafer Bars	143
Dream Bar Cake	144
Snickers Cake	145
Luscious Lava Nut Cake	146
Mickey's Peanut Butter Oatmeal	147
Oooie-gooie Chewies	148
Sherry's Chocolate Almond Cherry Pie Delight	149
No Bake Cookies	150
Becca's Peanut butter Oatey Oatmeal	151
Orange-Lemon Chocolate Kolaches	152
Banana S'moores	153
Armadillo Eggs	154
Strawberry Vanilla Chocolate Mama's	155
Raspberry-flavored Tootsie Pop Icing	156
Tippy's Coffee Balls	157
Holiday Fruity-Fruit	158
Cookie Cereal	159
Cookie Dough Ice Cream Cereal	160
Extra Sweet Honey Bun	161
Tippy's Tipperroo	162
Crunchy Peanut butter and Jelly Sandwich	163
Fried Peanut Butter and Jelly Sandwich	164
In-between Snack	165
Samantha's Chocolate Stuffed Surprise	166
Commissary Critters	167

Meals and Snacks

Columbian Rice

Contributed by: James A Millsaps

Ingredients

1 chili soup

1 pkg. Jalapeno pepper (culled & sliced)

1 tbsp. salad dressing

1 tbsp. soy sauce

1 pkg. ranch dressing

¼ bag instant rice

1 pkg. saltine crackers (optional)

Directions

Pre-heat a full hot pot of water to the 5-cup mark. In a hot pot insert, pour in crushed soup noodles and the entire seasoning pocket. Pour in jalapeno slices. Add the spoonful of salad dressing and the packet of ranch dressing. (If ranch dressing is not available just use another tbsp. of the salad dressing). Add water until the insert is about three quarter (¾) full. Add soy sauce and stir until the mixture is a uniform orange.

Slowly pour in the instant rice until it reaches just short of the brim. Add water slowly until the rice is covered. Carefully and slowly push the spoon down the sides, back and forth until the rice is blended with soup mixture. Pour in just a little more rice until you see the insert is near the top. Place in hot pot and put the lid on. Fill the hot pot with water and heat for forty-five (45) minutes to one (1) hour. After you transfer it to your bowl, it will look like three inserts worth of rice. Serve with crackers (optional). Makes 2 servings

Spicy Mackerel Rice

Contributed by: C. Dominguez

Ingredients

1 pkg. instant rice
1 pkg. pickle (sliced & diced)
1 bottle hot sauce
1 bag pork skins
3 pouches Jack Mack in water
¾ bottle jalapeno cheese
½ bag BBQ chips (crushed)
½ bag jalapeno chips (crushed)
½ bag corn chips (crushed)
10 packets sweetener

Directions

Place mackerels into hot pot to heat up. In two bowls split instant rice, add hot water only enough to top rice. Cover and let cook. Slightly crush pork skins adding the sliced and diced pickle, bottle of hot sauce, all of the sweeteners, close and shake and set aside.*

Uncover cooked rice and drain any excess water.

Open the mackerels and drain the water, then pour one and one half (1-½) of the mackerels into each bowl. Do one layer of jalapeno chips into each bowl, then do one layer of jalapeno cheese into each bowl, then one layer of BBQ chips into each bowl, then a layer of jalapeno cheese into each bowl, then a layer of corn chips into each bowl, then a layer of jalapeno cheese into each bowl.

Finally pour half of the set aside mixture * into each bowl.

Try to eat like a slice of cake so that you can taste all of the assorted flavors. Makes 2 to 4 servings.

Meals and Snacks

Nguyen's Fried Rice

Contributed by: J. Vu Nguyen

Ingredients

1 pkg. instant rice

1 pkg. pork skins

½ pkg. jalapeno chips

2 pkgs. Hot Fries

1 pkg. Mexican beef crumble

1 pkg. chili no beans

2 pkgs. soup seasoning (choice of flavor)

2 pkgs. jalapeno pepper (sliced) optional

1 pkg. chicken Vienna or 2 pkgs. Spam (diced)

Directions

Pour rice into bowl. Add soup seasoning, pour half of hot pot hot water over rice stir and cover for five (5) minutes, and then stir again. Let cook for thirty to forty-five minutes.

While waiting; heat up the chili no bean and Mexican beef pouches. Chop up the Vienna or Spam pouch and the jalapeno.

Crush the jalapeno chips, pork skins and Hot Fries. Pour all three into a large empty chip bag, and shake well;* after the rice is cooked add the Mexican beef and chili, stir well.

Add chopped meat and jalapeno peppers and stir well. Add crushed chips, pork skins and Hot Fries* mixture and stir well.   Makes 2 to 4 servings.

Dirty Rice

Contributed by: Tanner George Cummings

Ingredients

1 pkg. Mexican beef crumble

1 pkg. instant rice

2 pkgs. jalapeno peppers (sliced & diced)

1 pkg. beef flavored soup seasoning

1 pkg. ranch dressing (optional)

Black pepper

Hot sauce (optional)

Directions

Place Mexican beef crumble into hot pot to warm up. In a large bowl empty entire package of rice and add enough hot water to top of rice, stir and cover. While Mexican beef crumble is in hot pot open it up and pour in the beef flavored soup seasoning packet and stir. When rice is cooked pour Mexican beef crumble into rice and add the jalapeno peppers, black pepper, ranch dressing and hot sauce (if using). Stir and enjoy! Makes 2 servings.

Meals and Snacks

Cruzn Rice

Contributed by: Dela Cruz Frenando

Ingredients

1 pkg. instant rice

1 pkg. chicken flavored seasoning packet

2 tbsp. pickle juice

1 tbsp. Sevilla seasoning (coriander & annatto)

Directions

In a large bowl pour in the rice and add hot water to top rice and cover until the rice absorbs the water. Then add the rest of the ingredients and stir well.

Enjoy!

Cheap Chicken

Contributed by: Tanner George Cummings

Ingredients

1 pkg. chicken flavored soup (crushed)

2 squirts squeeze cheese

1 tbsp. salad dressing

1 pkg. ranch dressing

¼ pkg. instant rice

Hot sauce

Directions

In a large bowl, pour in the soup and rice. Add the hot water to cover the soup and rice. Stir and cover until the water is absorbed about five (5) minutes.

Add all the remaining ingredients, stir well and then enjoy! Makes 1 serving.

Meals and Snacks

Chicken Noodle Tortilla Soup

Contributed by: Terry Barnett

Ingredients

1 pkg. chicken Ramen noodle soup

½ pkg. chicken chunk

2 tbsp. salsa

12 tortilla chips (crushed)

2 squirts jalapeno cheese squeeze

2 mugs

Directions

Crush the package of chicken soup, split evenly between each mug. Add to each mug one quarter (1/4) package of chicken chunk, one tbsp. of salsa and one squirt of jalapeno squeeze cheese. Cover with hot water to one and one half (1-½) inches from the top, stir well. When noodles are soft, stir in crushed tortilla chips, enjoy!

Makes 2 servings.

Orange Chicken

Contributed by: William Terrell

Ingredients

1 pouch chicken chunk

1 cup instant rice

1 packet orange sports drink

1 packet chili seasoning

5 packets jalapeno peppers

Directions

Place a handful of rice, chicken, some of the seasoning packet, a few peppers and the orange sports drink into an empty chip bag. Let sit for one (1) hour, place into hot pot for two (2) hours to cook. Cook remaining rice. Mix the chicken mixture with the rice and let stand for five (5) minutes. Top with remaining peppers.

Enjoy! Makes 2 servings.

Lindsey's Ritzy Pate

Contributed by: Lance Lindsey

Ingredients

1 pkg. chicken chunk

1 pkg. Spam

1 pkg. mackerel

5 single serve pkgs. cream cheese

2 pkg. jalapeno peppers

1 pkg. French onion chips

1 pkg. snack crackers

2 tbsp. salad dressing (optional)

Directions

Dice and mince Spam, shred mackerel and add to Spam.* Crush the French onion chips to a fine powder and mix half of the bag with the above combo* in a bowl. Set aside to marinate.

In another bowl, dice the jalapenos. Shred chicken chunk and add to the jalapenos, squeeze cream cheese into the mix and stir.

Combine both bowls, thoroughly whisk together. Add 2 spoonfuls of salad dressing for a creamier taste. Spread on crackers and enjoy!

Meals and Snacks

Refried Beanie Chicken Winnies

Contributed by: Tanner George Cummings

Ingredients

½ pkg. instant refried beans

¼ bottle squeeze cheese

1 pkg. chicken Vienna Winnies

2 pkgs. jalapenos (diced)

1 sleeve saltine crackers

Corn chips

Directions

In a bowl, cut up the jalapeno peppers (if not already diced). Cover and set aside.

In another bowl cut up the chicken Vienna Winnies, pour into a bag; pour in two tbsp. of water and place in a hot pot to heat up.

Pour the ½ bag of instant refried beans into a bowl and add hot water while stirring. The beans should come out to a medium thickness.

Pull out the chicken Vienna Winnies and pour into the bowl with the instant refried beans, adding the jalapenos and squeeze cheese. Stir thoroughly. Eat with the saltines or corn chips and enjoy! Makes 1 serving.

Meals and Snacks

Chicken Salad

Contributed by: Merri Joy Lettining

Ingredients

1-2 pkg. chili flavored soup (crushed)

1 pkg. chicken chunk

1 pkg. jalapeno pepper (diced)

2 tbsp. sandwich spread

Squeeze cheese

Directions

Pour the soup with out the seasoning into a large bowl, add hot water to cover noodles, cover and let absorb the hot water.

Place chicken chunk into hot pot to heat up.

Uncover the noodles and add the chili seasoning, the diced jalapeno pepper, sandwich spread and squeeze cheese. Stir well.

Remove chicken chunk and open, drain any juices and pour into soup salad mixture, stir, cover and let cool down, one (1) hour. Enjoy!

Straight Strutten Chicken

Contributed by: Tanner George Cummings

Ingredients

1 pkg. chicken chunk

½ pkg. instant rice

1 pkg. chicken flavored soup seasoning packet

½ pkg. regular pickle (sliced & diced)

2 pkgs. jalapeno peppers (sliced & diced)

1 pkg. flour tortillas

3 tbsp. squeeze cheese

Onion flakes

Salsa

Directions

In a bag, open and pour in the chicken chunk, the pickle, the jalapeno peppers, a little bit of the onion flakes, a little bit of the salsa and mix well. Place into the hot pot for one (1) hour.

In a large bowl, pour in the ½ bag of instant rice and add hot water until rice has a slightly visible layer of water, cover and let rice absorb the hot water.

After five (5) minutes pour the chicken seasoning into the bowl of rice and stir.

Remove the chicken chunk mixture from the hot pot and pour into bowl of rice. Add some squeeze cheese and mix up the ingredients.

Put some on a tortilla and enjoy!

Sweet N Sour Chicken

Contributed by: Bill Nguyen

Ingredients

1 pkg. instant rice

1 pkg. chicken chunk

1 pkg. pork skins

1 pkg. chili flavored seasoning packet

2 tbsp. BBQ sauce

¼ tbsp. black pepper

½ pkg. lemon sports drink

1/3 cup water

Directions

Cook rice in the bag with very hot water. Mix other ingredients together and heat in a separate bag in the hot pot, until hot.

Divide the rice into two bowls and pour the mixture over the rice. Makes 2 servings.

Todd's Tasty Tacos

Contributed by: Todd Carman

Ingredients

1 pkg. instant refried beans or chili

1 pkg. flour tortillas

2 pkgs. jalapenos (diced)

1 bag pork skins, slightly crushed

1 pkg. summer sausage (optional) if using pork skins

¼ tsp. black pepper

Corn chips

Jalapeno cheese

Hot sauce

Salsa

Directions

Put beans, diced jalapeno peppers, pork skins, summer sausage and black pepper into a spread bowl. Add enough hot water (the hotter the better) to barely cover the beans. Cover the bowl with a newspaper and allow to cook for about ten (10) minutes.

While that is cooking, place the tortillas, two (2) at a time, on top of steaming hot pot to heat them up, flipping the pair after thirty (30) seconds. Place steamed tortillas in a separate bowl and cover.

When the beans are cooked-they should have the consistency of medium thickness refried beans-stir well. Pour 1/8 of a bag of corn chips on top of the beans. Shake a liberal amount of hot sauce onto the corn chips and mix well. Open up some tortillas, squeeze some jalapeno cheese on each tortilla, and then add a little salsa.

Fold tortillas and enjoy. Making 2 to 3 servings.

Jalapeno Beef Tacos

Contributed by: Tanner George Cummings

Ingredients

1 pkg. Mexican beef crumble

3 pkgs. jalapenos (sliced & diced)

½ pkg. instant refried beans

½ pkg. instant potatoes (four cheese or buttered)

1 pkg. tortillas

1 bottle squeeze cheese

Directions

Place the Mexican beef crumble into a hot pot and let heat up. Allow to heat for at least forty-five (45) minutes.

Pour the instant refried beans into a bowl; pour in hot water until covered. Stir until medium thick, cover and set aside.

In another bowl pour in the instant potatoes and add two (2) tablespoons of hot water and stir until thick.

Open the Mexican beef crumble and drain the grease off, and then pour into another bowl. Then take and mix all the instant refried beans, instant potatoes, jalapenos, and Mexican beef crumble together. Put some on a tortilla and squirt some squeeze cheese on top. Fold and roll. Eat and enjoy! Makes 2 servings.

Mystery Meat Tacos

Contributed by: F. Trevino

Ingredients

1 pkg. Mexican beef crumble

1 pkg. chili no beans

1 pkg. summer sausage

½ pkg. instant refried beans

3 pkgs. jalapeno peppers (sliced)

1 pkg. flour tortillas

Salsa

Squeeze cheese

Directions

In a bowl, slice the summer sausage into little pieces, pour them into a bag and place into the hot pot. Let them heat up for forty-five (45) minutes.

Put the Mexican beef crumble and chili no beans into the hot pot for forty-five (45) minutes.

Pour instant refried beans into a bowl and add hot water. Stir until medium thickness. Add a couple shots of salsa and the jalapenos to the instant refried beans. Pour in the chili no beans and stir.

Drain grease off of the Mexican beef crumble and pour into the mixture. Then throw in the summer sausage and stir well.

Put some on a tortilla with some squeeze cheese and enjoy! Makes 2 to 4 servings.

Tacos ala TDCJ

Contributed by: Jorge Manzano Gonsalez

Ingredients

1 pkg. flour tortillas

1 pkg. beef tips

1 bag potato chips (regular)

1 bag cheesy cheesers (regular)

3 pkgs. jalapeno peppers, to taste (optional)

Camino Real Cheese product (optional) any flavor squeeze cheese can be used

Prepared refried beans (optional)

Directions

Place all dry ingredients in a plastic bag. Crush the chips. Add water until chips are saturated. Add beef tips to the bag mixture. Place bag with the mixture into a hot pot and heat up the mixture while making sure the gravy juice is always at the top of the mixture.

Add water if needed to keep the top of the mixture juicy. Cook up to one (1) hour. Place mixture into each tortilla and top with refried beans. Enjoy! Makes 2 to 4 servings.

Meals and Snacks

Breakfast Tacos

Contributed by: Tanner George Cummings

Ingredients

1 pkg. flour tortillas

3 eggs

½ pkg. instant potatoes

½ pkg. instant refried beans

1 bottle squeeze cheese

1 bottle salsa (to taste)

Directions

In a rice bag crack open the eggs and stir, then place in hot pot and stir until eggs are scrambled.

In a large bowl pour the half bag of instant potatoes and enough hot water to make them thick. In another bowl pour the half bag of instant refried beans and add enough hot water to create a medium thickness.

Then on a tortilla put a layer of squeeze cheese then some eggs, potatoes, beans and salsa.

Makes four to eight tacos enjoy!

Meals and Snacks

Chicken Tacos

Contributed by: Tanner George Cummings

Ingredients

1 pkg. chicken flavored seasoning

½ pkg. instant refried beans

½ pkg. instant rice

1 pkg. chicken chunk

3 pkg. jalapeno peppers (sliced & diced)

1 pkg. flour tortillas

1 bottle squeeze cheese

Directions

Pour the half package of instant refried beans in one bowl; add hot water to top of refried beans. Cover and set aside.

In another bowl, pour the half package of instant rice and add hot water to top of instant rice. Cover and set aside.

Place chicken chunk into hot pot to heat up. Make sure to open the package and mix the chicken seasoning into the package, stir and let heat up.

When chicken chunk is ready drain juices and pour in the bowl with the rice, mix in the jalapeno peppers and stir well.

Then on a tortilla put some squeeze cheese, some instant refried beans, some chicken rice mixture and fold like tacos, then enjoy!

Meals and Snacks

Fantastic Fish Tacos

Contributed by: Todd Carman

Ingredients

3 pkgs. soups, crushed

1 pkg. pork skins, slightly crushed

½ spoonful black pepper

2 spoonful dehydrated onion

2 pkgs. lemon cool down

2 pkgs. sweetener

1 pkg. chicken seasoning

1 pkg. chili seasoning

1-2 pkgs. Jack mackerels (in water). 1 pkg. tuna

2 pkgs. jalapeno peppers (diced)

½ pkg. pickles (diced)

2 spoonfuls pickle juice

1 heaping spoonful mustard

1 heaping spoonful relish

3 heaping spoonful salad dressing

¼- ½ pkg. corn chips

1 pkg. flour tortillas

Hot sauce (optional)

Directions

Mix the crushed soups, pork skins, black pepper, dehydrated onion, lemon cool down, sweetener, chicken seasoning and chili seasoning together into a large spread bowl; add hot water (almost two-thirds (2/3) of the hot pot), cover and let set for almost ten (10) minutes.

Uncover bowl and stir the mix (it should be moist).

Add the next eight ingredients (mackerels, tuna, jalapeno peppers, pickle, pickle juice, mustard, relish and salad dressing) stir well.

Add corn chips to taste, stir to mix.

Serve on tortillas, top with hot sauce.

Makes three to four servings

Meals and Snacks

Tippy's Spicy Tuna Wraps

Contributed by: Kristin Metz

Ingredients

1 pkg. tuna

1 pkg. flour tortillas (4 tortillas)

2 pkgs. jalapeno peppers (sliced & diced)

½ pkg. hot pickle (sliced & diced)

1 pkg. chili flavored soup (crushed)

¼ bottle squeeze cheese

Jalapeno chips (crushed)

Directions

Cook noodles without seasoning in a spread bowl. Drain the water off of the tuna and pour into another large spread bowl, and then break up into flakes/pieces.

Then mix the noodles with the seasoning, tuna, jalapeno pepper, pickle and crushed jalapeno chips (as much chips as desired) and stir. Then mix in the one quarter (1/4) squeeze cheese and stir.

Place the mixture into the four (4) flour tortillas and place into a doubled bagged cooking bag, and place into hot pot for thirty (30) minutes. Enjoy!

Tamales

Contributed by: Bill Nguyen

Ingredients

2 pkgs. chili no beans

2 pkgs. summer sausage (chopped)

2 pkgs. pork skins, crushed

3 pkgs. jalapeno peppers (finely chopped)

¾ pkg. tortilla chips

Dehydrated onion flakes seasoning

Garlic powder (seasoning)

Supplies

Empty soup bags

Cooking bags (empty chip bags)

Directions

Meat filling: Mix both packets of chili no beans, the chopped sausage and chopped jalapeno peppers together and heat. Crush the pork skins and set aside. After the meat is warmed up, pour into a bowl and add the crushed pork skins, mix well.

Masa: Crush tortilla chips to a fine powder; add some dehydrated onion seasoning and some garlic powder. Add warm water to the tortilla chip powder a little at a time, knead into dough. Should be about like cookie dough. The dough should be sticky but not so sticky it sticks to your fingers.

Final preparation: Take a small ball of Masa (about golf ball size) and spread out flat on a soup bag, which has been opened up flat (work on only half of the soup bag). Use the other half of the bag to help spread the Masa out. (To make the Masa into a rectangle about four (4) inches wide by five (5) inches long and about one- eighth (1/8) inches thick.) Put a spoonful of meat mixture on the top of the four (4) inch wide side of the Masa, roll up Masa, but do not let the bag roll into the Masa (the bag is used as a guide to shape). After the tamale is rolled up, bring back to the end of the bag. Now bag and tamale together, close off one end of the bag. Place tamale roll, closed end down in a cooking bag. Place cooking bags in hot pot for two hours. Then remove from hot pot and carefully eat while hot! Tasty huh!

Meals and Snacks

Cheesy Chicken Burritos

Contributed by: Erica Anthony

Ingredients

1 pkg. chicken chunk

½ bag instant rice

1 bag jalapeno chips (crushed)

Pkg. chicken soup seasoning

6-8 flour tortillas

¼ bottle squeeze cheese

Directions

Finely shred the chicken.

Cook rice until tender.

Mix in the shredded chicken, jalapeno chips, squeeze cheese and chicken soup seasoning and mix well. Then place on top of tortilla and enjoy!

Makes 6-8 burritos

Meals and Snacks

Chipotle Chicken & Ranch Burritos

Contributed by: Ceyma Bina

Ingredients

1 pkg. chicken chunk

5-6 heaping tbsp. of crushed jalapeno chips

1 pkg. jalapeno pepper (chopped & seeded)

1 pkg. chili seasoning

1 pkg. ranch dressing

1 bottle squeeze cheese

6 flour tortillas

Several dashes of hot sauce

Directions

Pour chicken into a bowl and separate the chunks with a spoon. Add the crushed jalapeno chips, the jalapeno peppers, the chili seasoning, the ranch dressing and the hot sauce. Mix well. Add the squeeze cheese to the tortillas and top with the chicken mixture. Roll into burritos and place into a chip bag. Cook in hot pot for forty-five (45) minutes.

Makes 6 servings.

Spicy Chicken Burrito

Contributed by: Jennifer Olvera

Ingredients

1 pkg. chicken chunk

1 pkg. chili flavored soup

1 pkg. flour tortillas

½ pkg. salsa Verde chips (crushed)

½ pkg. plain potato chips (3 oz.)

¼ cup instant rice

2 tbsp. mayonnaise or salad dressing

1 pkg. jalapeno pepper (diced)

1 pkg. chicken flavored seasoning packet

Squeeze cheese

Hot sauce (optional)

Directions

Crush up the noodle soup reserving the seasoning packet, then pour the crushed soup noodles into a bag adding the one-quarter (1/4) cup of rice. Add one (1) cup of hot water from hot pot and let cook for five (5) minutes. Drain the chicken chunk pouch. Place the noodle mixture in a bowl and add the mayonnaise or salad dressing, chicken seasoning and mix. Then add chips, chicken, jalapenos, two (2) squirts of squeeze cheese and mix together. Place the mixture on a flour tortilla, add hot sauce (optional) and roll like a burrito. Enjoy! Makes 4 servings.

Meals and Snacks

Mexican Pizza

Contributed by: Merri Joy Lettining

Ingredients

½ pkg. corn chips

1 cup instant refried beans

1 cheese curls (smashed)

2 pkg. jalapeno peppers (sliced)

1 pkg. summer sausage (sliced)

Dehydrated onion

Squeeze cheese

Directions

Mix corn chips into Masa (paste) with water until it has thick dough like consistency.

Spread the Masa out on an open chip bag in rectangle form approximately twelve (12) inches by eight (8) inches. Prepare beans and spread over Masa.

Add hot water and two (2) squeezes of cheese to cheese curls; mix into desired consistency and spread over beans, a spoonful at a time. Spread the sliced jalapenos and sliced summer sausage over the top. Sprinkle on the dehydrated onion.

Slice pizza into desired number of pieces and cook in hot pot.

Makes up to 8 slices

Meals and Snacks

Chili Pizza

Contributed by: Tanner George Cummings

Ingredients

2 pkgs. chili soups

1 pkg. chili no beans pouch

2 pkgs. jalapenos (sliced)

2 tbsp. salad dressing

¼ bottle squeeze cheese

1 handful cheese puffs (crushed)

1 large chip bag

Directions

Take both of the chili soups and crush them up and pour into the large chip bag along with the chili seasoning packs. Add approximately one-half (1/2) to three quarters (3/4) cup of hot water and mix well. Flatten down fold open end, cover and let set- this will be the crust. Place chili no beans pouch into hot pot and let reheat for about twenty (20) to thirty (30) minutes.

Then at the center of the large bag, cut all the way down and cut the bottom edge from corner to corner. Take chili no beans pouch and open up, set aside. Then spread the salad dressing over the top of the pizza. Pour the chili no beans over the top and spread out evenly. Pour squeeze cheese over the top and then top it off with crushed cheese puffs.

Take your spoon and divide in half. Makes two servings

Meals and Snacks

Poor Man's Pizza

Contributed by: Tanner George Cummings

Ingredients

1 pkg. beef flavored soup (crushed)

¼ bag instant refried beans

1 pkg. nacho chips (crushed)

1 pkg. jalapeno (sliced)

1 tbsp. salad dressing

Squeeze cheese

Cheese puffs (slightly crushed)

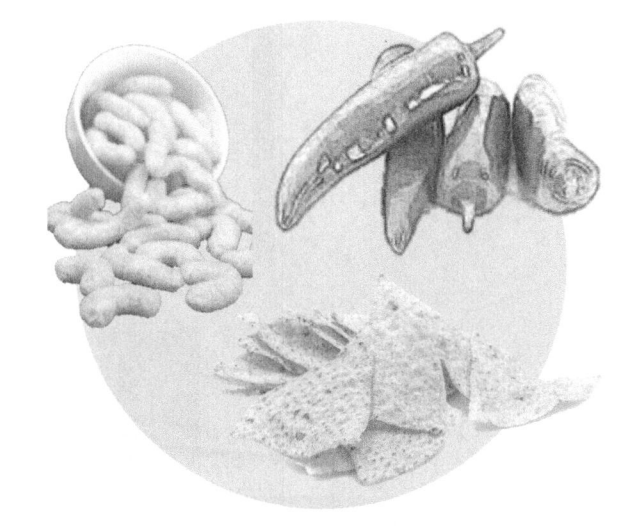

Directions

Pour the beef soup with the seasoning into the nacho chip bag and the instant refried beans. Add hot water to cover ingredients. Mix thoroughly. Fold the top, lay down flat and flatten evenly. Cover and let soak up the hot water, for about five (5) minutes.

Then cut open down the length of the bag and at the bottom from corner to corner to completely open the pizza.

Layer the top with the one (1) tablespoon of salad dressing then the squeeze cheese and then add the cheese puffs and jalapenos. Eat and enjoy!

Makes one serving

Meals and Snacks

Tuna Pizza

Contributed by: Tanner George Cummings

Ingredients

2 pkgs. chicken soups (crushed)

1 pkg. tuna

1 tbsp. salad dressing

2 tbsp. squeeze cheese

1 large chip bag

Handful corn chips

Directions

Pour the two (2) chicken soups with seasoning into a large empty chip bag, add in enough hot water to cover the soups, mix well.

Fold top of chip bag then lay down flat, flatten as evenly as possible then cover and let the soup soak up the hot water. Leave for about five (5) minutes. Cut the chip bag down the center and from corner to corner to completely open up the pizza.

Spread the one (1) tablespoon of salad dressing over the pizza. Open the tuna and drain off the water then pour over the top of the pizza. Spread the squeeze cheese over the top and top off with the corn chips. Eat and enjoy!

Meals and Snacks

Jack Mack Pizza

Contributed by: Tanner George Cummings

Ingredients

1 pkg. chicken soup (crushed)

1 pkg. Jack Mackerel

¼ pkg. instant rice

1 bag cheese curls (crushed)

½ tube ranch dressing

Corn chips

1 large empty chip bag

Squeeze cheese

Directions

Pour crushed soup with the seasoning, crushed cheese curls and instant rice into empty large chip bag, add enough hot water to just cover the ingredients. Fold the top and mix well. Then lay down flat, flatten down evenly, cover and let the pizza soak up the hot water for about five (5) minutes.

Cut the bag completely open from the top to the bottom in the center and again from the bottom corner to corner.

Pour half of the tube of the ranch dressing all over the top, then the squeeze cheese and some corn chips.

Open the Jack Mackerel and drain the juices and then pour on top. Top it off with more corn chips. Enjoy!

Meals and Snacks

Spam Pizza

Contributed by: Tanner George Cummings

Ingredients

1 pkg. chili soup (crushed)

1 pkg. Spam (sliced into cubes)

1 pkg. nacho chips (crushed)

1 tbsp. salad dressing

Squeeze cheese

Corn chips (crushed)

Hot sauce

Directions

In a large empty chip bag, place chili soup and seasoning into the bag. Pour in the corn chips and add enough hot water to cover the soup and chips. Mix thoroughly making sure the seasoning does not sink to the corners. Fold top, lay down flat, flatten down evenly then cover and let soak up hot water, about five (5) minutes.

Put Spam cubes in a bag and place in hot pot to heat up. Cut open the bag from top center down to the bottom and cut from bottom corner to corner. Spread the salad dressing on top, then the Spam and the Nacho chips. Top off with the squeeze cheese and hot sauce. Enjoy!

Makes one serving

Sardine Pizza

Contributed by: Tanner George Cummings

Ingredients

1 pkg. chili flavored soup

1 pkg. sardines in Louisiana hot sauce

¼ pkg. instant refried beans

1 pkg. nacho chips (crushed)

1 pkg. jalapeno pepper (sliced & diced)

½ pkg. ranch dressing

1 soup bag of crushed cheese puffs

2 tbsp. squeeze cheese

1 large empty chip bag

Directions

Place the crushed soup with seasoning, refried beans and crushed nacho chips into the large empty chip bag and add enough hot water to cover contents and mix thoroughly so that the seasoning does not sink down to the corners. Fold the top and lay flat, flatten down evenly, then cover and let soak up the hot water for five (5) minutes.

Place sardine pouch into the hot pot to heat up for about twenty (20) to twenty-five (25) minutes. Cut open the chip bag from top center down to the bottom center and then from bottom corner to corner. Spread over the top the half (1/2) tube of ranch dressing, the crushed cheese puffs and the squeeze cheese.

Open up the sardine pouch and pour on top, then top it off with the jalapenos. Eat and enjoy!

Meals and Snacks

Chili Beef Tips Pizza

Contributed by: Jonathon Asher

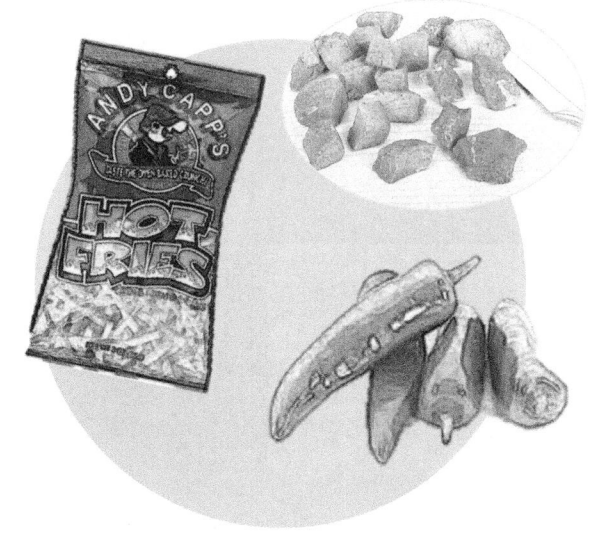

Ingredients

1 pkg. jalapeno chips

1 pkg. BBQ chips

1 pkg. instant refried beans

2 pkgs. Hot fries

1 pkg. chili with beans

1 pkg. beef tips

1 bottle of squeeze cheese

1 pkg. pickle (dill-regular)

1 pkg. jalapeno pepper

2 pkgs. ranch dressing

2 pkgs. nacho chips

1 pkg. instant potatoes

1 large empty chip bag

Directions

Makes one serving Crush up the BBQ chips and the jalapeno chips and pour your desired amount of each into the large empty chip bag. Add half (1/2) package of instant refried beans and both packages of Hot fries. Add hot water until you have reached your desired texture. Place on a flat surface and flatten down, fold top once or twice, cover and set aside and let cook.

While the pizza is cooking; put the beef tips and chili with beans into the hot pot to heat up. Then next dice up the jalapenos peppers and the pickle. Once the pizza is cooked, cut the bag from top to bottom down the center. Then cut the bottom from corner to corner. Put some squeeze cheese on top and spread around. Pour on the chili. Next, pour the instant potatoes into a bowl and add hot water, stir, cover and let cook. Once the potatoes are cooked, spread them over the top of the chili and add the beef tips. Add more squeeze cheese, the pickle and jalapenos to the top. Finally add the ranch dressing to the top and add the nacho chips (crushed) over the top. Eat and

Mexican Beef Crumble Pizza

Contributed by: Tanner George Cummings

Ingredients

1 pkg. Mexican beef crumble pouch

3 pkgs. beef flavored soups (crushed)

½ pkg. instant refried beans

4 pkgs. jalapeno peppers (sliced & diced)

¼ bottle squeeze cheese

1 tbsp. salad dressing

1 tbsp. ketchup

Cheese puffs (slightly crushed)

1 large empty chip bag

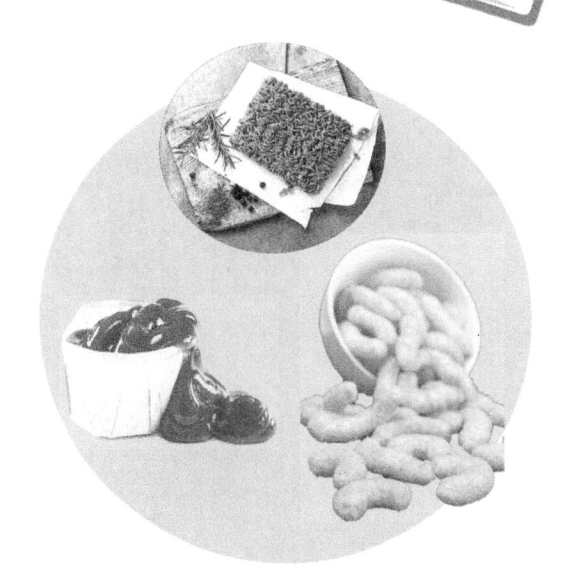

Directions

Pour the beef soups and seasoning into the large empty chip bag; pour in the instant refried beans. Pour in hot water to the top of the soup and beans. Mix well to spread the beef seasoning thoroughly. Carefully fold the top of bag, lay down flat as evenly as possible, cover and let soak up the hot water.

Place Mexican beef crumble pouch into hot pot and let heat up for twenty (20) to twenty-five (25) minutes. Next cut open the chip bag from top to bottom down the center then cut from the bottom corner across to the other corner to completely open the bag. (There should be no water or juices remaining). Pour on the top and spread the one tablespoon of salad dressing. Remove the Mexican beef crumble pouch from the hot pot. (Careful it's hot!) Open and drain grease from the pouch and spread the beef over the top of the pizza.

Sprinkle the slightly crushed cheese puffs and the sliced and diced jalapenos on top, and then top it off with squeeze cheese. Enjoy! Makes two to four servings.

Killer Frito Pie

Contributed by: James Clayton

Ingredients

1 pkg. chili

1 squirt cheese

1 bag corn chips

1 pkg. jalapeno peppers

1 pkg. instant refried beans

Directions

Take a bag of chili and wash it off. Set it up in your hot pot and open it at the very top. Put three (3) spoonfuls of water in the chili. Put a squirt of cheese in the chili and let it cook. Let it cook for about thirty (30) minutes and stir. Put about a third (1/3) to half (1/2) a bag of instant refried beans in a large bowl, add water and while the beans are cooking, cut the jalapeno peppers up and then add them. When the beans are ready, spread a layer of corn chips on top, and then spread the chili on top of that.

Makes two servings.

Frito Pie

Contributed by: Merri Joy Lettining

Ingredients

1 - ½ cups corn chips

1 pkg. cheese curls

½ pkg. instant refried beans

1 pkg. jalapeno pepper (diced)

Squeeze cheese

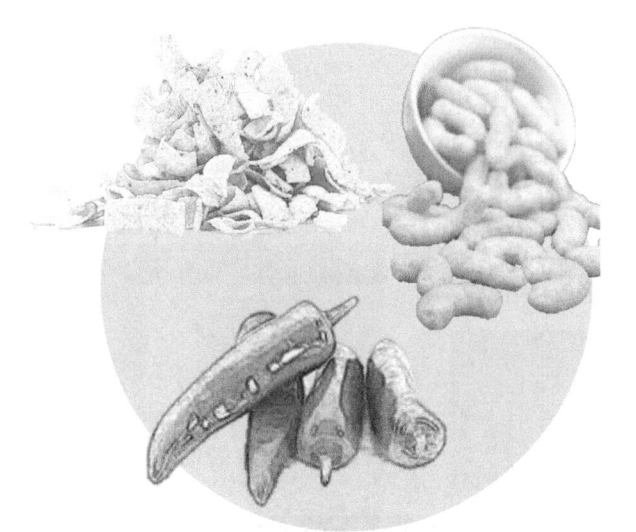

Directions

Pour the beans into a bowl and add hot water to cover beans, stir and cover for five (5) minutes. Pour the corn chips and cheese curls into another bowl. Uncover beans and pour on top of chips. Sprinkle the diced jalapeno peppers on top. Finally add the desired amount of squeeze cheese. Enjoy!

Meals and Snacks

Chicken Chili Nachos

Contributed by: James Cotter

Ingredients

1-2 pkgs. chicken chili

1 bag instant refried beans

1 bag salsa Verde chips (crushed)

1 bottle squeeze cheese

1 bag tortilla chips or corn chips

Directions

Heat chicken chili pouches in hot pot. In a bowl, prepare instant refried beans to desired thickness. Pour tortilla or corn chips into another bowl for the bottom layer. Mix in the chicken chili and the crushed salsa Verde chips into the refried beans and mix well. Then pour over the top of the tortilla or corn chips. Pour some squeeze cheese on top and enjoy!

Meals and Snacks

Sharp Cheddar Chicken Nachos

Contributed by: Quintasha Harris

Ingredients

1 pkg. chicken chunk (shredded)

¼ pkg. cheese puffs (crushed)

¼ bottle squeeze cheese

¼ cup hot water

1 pkg. jalapeno peppers (chopped)

2 pkg. cream cheese

½ pkg. tortilla chips

Directions

Crush cheese puffs and pour into insert cup. Add bottle cheese with water, mix well. Add additional water or cheese puffs for desired texture. Place shredded chicken and cheese sauce in a small bag, cook in hot pot for thirty (30) to forty-five (45) minutes. Meanwhile, chop jalapenos and put tortilla chips in a bowl. When the sauce is ready, pour it over chips. Sprinkle with chopped peppers and cream cheese.

Makes two servings.

Meals and Snacks

Chili Cheese Nachos

Contributed by: Tanner George Cummings

Ingredients

2 pkg. chili no beans (pouches)

1 bag tortilla chips

½ bottle squeeze cheese

Directions

Place the cleaned chili no beans pouches into hot pot and fill with water heating for one (1) hour. Next open the bag of tortilla chips at the top, down the center and from corner to corner at the bottom. Keeping the tortilla chips on the bag lay down on table or flat surface where you plan to eat. Next remove the chili no beans pouches, open and pour over the tortilla chips evenly. Pour the squeeze cheese evenly over the top and enjoy!

Makes two servings.

Jalapeno Cheese Nachos

Contributed by: Tanner George Cummings

Ingredients

5 pkgs. jalapeno peppers (sliced & diced)

½ bottle squeeze cheese

½ bag tortilla chips

Directions

Place the half (1/2) bottle of squeeze cheese into the hot pot and let heat up.

In a bowl, pour in tortilla chips, spread out jalapenos, and then pour the squeeze cheese on top.

Makes two servings.

Meals and Snacks

Beef -n- Cheese Nachos

Contributed by: Tanner George Cummings

Meals and Snacks

Ingredients

1 pkg. Mexican beef crumble

½ bottle squeeze cheese

½ bag tortilla chips

Directions

Put the Mexican beef crumble into the hot pot and let heat up for about forty-five (45) minutes. Place the half (1/2) bottle squeeze cheese into another hot pot to heat up. Pour tortilla chips into a bowl. Drain the grease off the Mexican beef crumble and pour on top of the tortilla chips, and then top off with the squeeze cheese. Enjoy!

Makes two servings.

Simple Sardines

Contributed by: Tanner George Cummings

Ingredients

1 pkg. sardines

1 pkg. chili flavored soup (crushed)

1 tbsp. ketchup

1 pkg. Jalapeno peppers (sliced & diced)

½ sleeve saltine crackers

1 tbsp. squeeze cheese

Directions

In a large spread bowl, cook the soup. Once that is cooked add in the sardines, ketchup, jalapeno pepper, and the squeeze cheese. Stir and enjoy with the saltine crackers.

Makes one serving.

Sardine Spread

Contributed by: Tanner George Cummings

Ingredients

1 pkg. chicken soup

1 sleeve saltine crackers

1 pkg. jalapeno pepper (sliced & diced)

½ pickle (sliced & diced)

¼ bag instant refried beans

¼ bag instant rice

1 tbsp. ketchup

1 pouch sardines in Louisiana hot sauce

2 tbsp. jalapeno cheese

1 handful corn chips

Directions

Crunch up the chicken soup, pour into a bowl and add the instant beans and rice; pour on just enough hot water to cover the mixture. Place cover on bowl and let cook for five (5) minutes. Uncover the bowl and pour in sardines, jalapeno cheese, ketchup, pickle, jalapeno pepper, chicken seasoning and corn chips, mixing well. Eat with crackers.

Makes one serving.

Meals and Snacks

Slightly Sweet Nuttier Chicken

Contributed by: Tanner George Cummings

Ingredients

¼ pkg. instant rice

1 pkg. chicken flavored soup, (crushed)

¼ pkg. instant refried beans

1 tbsp. BBQ sauce

1 tbsp. hot sauce

1 tbsp. peanut butter

1-2 squeeze cheese

Directions

In a large spread bowl, pour the rice, the beans and the chicken soup (without the seasoning) into the bowl. Add hot water to cover the beans, rice and soup; cover and let mixture absorb the hot water for about five (5) minutes. After the five (5) minutes uncover and add remaining ingredients, stir and enjoy!

Meals and Snacks

Poor Man's Spread

Contributed by: Tanner George Cummings

Ingredients

1 soup (any flavor)

¼ bag instant rice

¼ bag instant refried beans

Directions

Crunch up soup (without the seasoning) and pour into a bowl. Add the instant rice and instant refried beans pouring in enough hot water to cover ingredients. Cover and let cook for five (5) minutes.

Uncover pour seasoning packet into bowl, mix well and enjoy!

Makes one serving.

Sweet -n- Sour Noodles

Contributed by: David B. Hayes

Ingredients

1 pkg. chili flavored soup (crushed)

1 can orange/pineapple juice

1 pkg. trail mix

1 pkg. hot peanuts

1 pkg. jalapeno pepper (sliced & seeds removed)

½ pickle (sliced)

½ cup salad dressing

½ cup squeeze cheese (or much as you want)

1 pkg. tortillas (flour)

Hot sauce (to taste)

Your choice of: meat, fish, chicken or pork

Directions

Pop the top of the can of orange/pineapple juice and set can in hot pot. Add water around the can until it almost floats and heat up the juice. Place the crushed chili flavored soup noodles in a large bowl. Pour hot juice over noodles; cover and let noodles soften for about fifteen (15) minutes or so. After the noodles have absorbed all the juice, mix in salad dressing, cheese and soup seasoning; stir until it has a mac-and-cheese texture. Add remaining ingredients (the trail mix, hot peanuts, jalapeno pepper, pickle and choice of protein) gradually while stirring well. Let sit, covered, for thirty (30) minutes so the flavors can blend. Spread mixture on the flour tortillas add the hot sauce to taste and enjoy!

Makes two to four servings.

Meals and Snacks

Sweet -n- Sour Bowl

Contributed by: James Cavazos

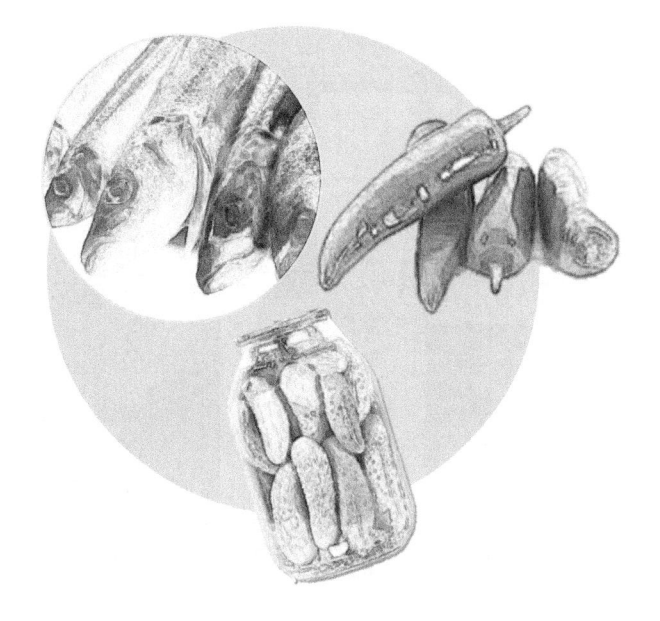

Ingredients

1 pkg. Jack Mackerel

3 pkgs. sweetener

2 pkgs. beef soup

1 tbsp. sandwich spread

3 tbsp. pickle juice

1 tbsp. heaping spoonfuls each of diced pickles and jalapeno peppers

1 pkg. pork skins

3 tbsp. BBQ sauce

Directions

To make sauce, add pickle juice, diced pickles & jalapenos, beef soup seasoning packets, sweeteners, BBQ sauce, sandwich spread and the oil from the Jack Mackerel pouch into a hot pot insert cup and stir. Heat the hot pot stirring occasionally. In another hot pot, heat water until very hot. Break each soup into four pieces and cook the noodles. Put pork skins into a bowl. Drain any left over water from the noodles and pour it over the pork skins. Cover the bowl and let stand for several minutes. Pour the sauce mixture over the noodles and toss lightly to coat all the noodles. Eat and enjoy!

Lemon Fish Flips

Contributed by: Flip Alapour

Ingredients

1 pkg. Picante beef soup

1 pouch Jack Mackerel

1 pkg. Lemon cool off

½ tbsp. garlic seasoning

2 tbsp. onion flakes

2 tbsp. strawberry preserves (optional)*

Meals and Snacks

Directions

Place all ingredients in a large empty chip bag. Shake up ingredients and add enough hot water to cover three-quarters (3/4) of the mixture. Tie off chip bag and place in hot pot to cook for thirty (30) minutes. Empty contents of bag into a bowl and enjoy! * For a different type of flavor, top off the meal with the strawberry preserves (jelly).

Wicked Popcorn Soup

Contributed by: K. Robinson

Ingredients

¾ can V8 juice

½ bag popcorn

1 pkg. pickle (chopped)

1 pkg. jalapeno pepper (chopped)

¼ bag Jalapeno chips (crushed)

1 pkg. chili seasoning

Directions

Mix the V8, pickle, jalapeno pepper, chili seasoning. Then add in the popcorn and the jalapeno chips. Mix well. Enjoy!

Meals and Snacks

No Meat Spread

Contributed by: Tanner George Cummings

Ingredients

¼ bag instant rice

¼ bag refried beans

¼ bottle salsa

1 tbsp. salad dressing

Dash hot sauce

Directions

Pour the beans and rice into a bowl and barely cover with hot water. Stir and cover and let set for five (5) minutes. Uncover after five (5) minutes and add the salsa, salad dressing and hot sauce. Stir up the ingredients. Enjoy!

Meals and Snacks

Hot Buttered Soup

Contributed by: Tanner George Cummings

Ingredients

1 pkg. chicken soup (crushed)

1 tbsp. peanut butter

1 tsp. hot sauce

Directions

Cook the soup for three (3) to five (5) minutes. Then add the peanut butter and hot sauce, mix and enjoy!

Meals and Snacks

Simply Scrumptious Ham Mac -n- Cheese

Contributed by: David B. Hayes

Ingredients

1 pkg. chicken flavored soup (crushed)

2 pkgs. Spam (cubed) or (1 Mexican beef or 1 chicken chunk may be substituted in place of Spam)

1 pkg. jalapeno pepper (seeded & diced)

¼ sleeve saltine crackers

¼ cup salad dressing

½ cup squeeze cheese

½ tsp. salt

1 tsp. black pepper

Hot sauce (optional)

Directions

In a covered bowl, cook crushed noodles in very hot water for a least a half hour, allowing for the noodles to absorb as much water as possible. Stir, drain and rinse the noodles. Combine the salad dressing, cheese, soup seasoning packet, jalapeno pepper, salt and black pepper with the noodles, stirring continuously until a nice Mac-n-cheese consistency is achieved; more cheese may be added if desired.

Add the Spam or substitute meat pouch. Stir well. Crush the saltines and sprinkle on top of the noodle mixture. Add additional salt & pepper or hot sauce if desired. Enjoy!

Makes two servings.

Commix

Contributed by: Tanner George Cummings

Ingredients

1 pkg. instant rice

1 pkg. beef flavored seasoning

1 pkg. Mexican beef crumble

1 pkg. summer sausage (sliced & diced)

1 pkg. chicken chunk

1pkg. mackerel in water (water drained)

1 pkg. regular pickle (sliced & diced)

3 pkgs. jalapeno pickles (sliced & diced)

1 pkg. salsa Verde chips (partly crushed)

½ bottle of squeeze cheese

1 pkg. ranch dressing

1 pkg. flour tortillas (optional)

1 sleeve saltine crackers (optional)

Directions

In a bowl, pour the entire bag of rice, add hot water, cover and let absorb the hot water. Heat up the Mexican beef crumble, summer sausage, and chicken chunk. Once they are nice and hot, drain the grease off the Mexican beef crumble and water off the chicken chunk and pour all three into the bowl with rice and stir. Mix in the beef soup seasoning packet, jalapeno pickles, regular pickle, ranch dressing and salsa Verde chips and stir.

Use flour tortillas or saltine crackers with the Commix and enjoy!

Meals and Snacks

Tasty Spuds

Contributed by: Tanner George Cummings

Ingredients

1 pkg. instant potatoes

1 pkg. ranch dressing

2 tbsp. instant powdered milk

1 tbsp. margarine/butter

Salt

Black pepper

Directions

In a large bowl with hot water, cook the instant potatoes. Add the ranch dressing, milk, and margarine/butter and stir well. Add some salt and pepper to taste stir and enjoy!

Meals and Snacks

Potato Salad

Contributed by: Tanner George Cummings

Ingredients

1 pkg. instant potatoes (any flavor)

6 boiled eggs (chopped)

1 tbsp. mustard

1-½ tbsp. salad dressing

4 tbsp. pickle (sliced & diced & chopped)

2 tbsp. squeeze cheese

Directions

In a large bowl, pour in the entire package of instant potatoes and add hot water a little at a time and stir until nice and thick. Then add the chopped boiled eggs, mustard, salad dressing, pickles and squeeze cheese. Stir together and then enjoy!

Makes two servings.

Meals and Snacks

Potato Cake

Contributed by: Stephanie Nix

Ingredients

1 pkg. plain potato chips (3 oz. bag)

¼ cup party mix chips

¼ cup instant rice

¼ cup instant refried beans

¼ cup corn chips

1 pkg. ranch dressing

Squeeze cheese

Hot sauce

Directions

Crush plain potato chips and party mix chips in an empty bag, then add rice, beans and add enough hot water to cover all of the ingredients. Close bag, place in a towel and wrap up to cook for two (2) or three (3) minutes. Place the potato chip mixture in a bowl, spread on the squeeze cheese and ranch dressing. Garnish with the corn chips and hot sauce. Enjoy!

Meals and Snacks

Jeff's Spaghetti Daze

Contributed by: Jeff Goddard

Ingredients

1 pkg. chili no beans

1 can V8 juice

2/3 bottle ketchup

2 heaping spoonful garlic (more or less to

2-3 heaping spoonful onion flakes

2 pkg. jalapeno peppers (diced)

1 pkg. summer sausage (diced)

3 pkg. chili flavored soup

1/3 - 1/2 pkg. jalapeno cheese puffs

Black pepper

Directions

Place the first seven (7) ingredients (chili no bean, V8, ketchup, garlic, onion flakes, jalapeno peppers, and summer sausage) into an empty corn chip bag. Add one-half (1/2)

cup of water and one (1) chili favored seasoning packet; and stir well. Place bag into hot pot and cook for forty-five (45) minutes to one (1) hour.

Put two (2) soups and one (1) chili seasoning packet into three separate bowls. Add hot water and cover for eight (8) to ten (10) minutes. Drain any excess water from the three (3) bowls and sprinkle black pepper on the noodles to taste.

Remove spaghetti sauce bag from hot pot, stir and pour evenly over the three (3) bowls of noodles.

Pour crushed jalapeno cheese puffs over the spaghetti sauce, mix well. Serve with snack crackers or saltines. (Optional). Makes three servings.

Prisagna (prison lasagna)

Contributed by: H. Nabilsi

Ingredients

2 pkg. beef flavored soups

2 pkg. Mexican beef crumble

4 pkg. cream cheese

8 oz. squeeze cheese

¾ can V8 juice

1 tbsp. habanero hot sauce

½ tsp. salt

2 oz. Ketchup

Dash, garlic ground

Dash, ground black pepper

Directions

Mix the half (1/2) tsp salt, dash garlic, dash pepper with the beef crumbles and mix well. Place in a bag and heat in a hot pot for one (1) hour. Put the two (2) soups (unbroken) in a bowl and add one seasoning packet and three-quarters (3/4) of a cup of hot water and cover and let cook.

Open up the can of V8 juice and heat three-quarters (3/4) of it in a second hot pot. In a second bowl, spread one fourth (1/4) of the soup noodles, top with half (1/2) of the meat mixture and spread evenly. Next cover with four (4) ounces of squeeze cheese and evenly spread. Cover the cheese layer with one half (1/2) of the remaining noodles. Top with the other half (1/2) of the meat mixture and spread evenly. Squeeze the four (4) cream cheeses over the meat layer. Then cover with the remaining noodles. Cover them with the remaining squeeze cheese. Mix the other seasoning packet with the habanero hot sauce, the 2 ounces of ketchup and the heated V8 juice and pour over the top of the main dish.

Cover and let stand for twenty (20) minutes. Makes two to three servings.

Meals and Snacks

Stuffed Jalapenos

Contributed by: Brandy Reese

Ingredients

½ pkg. chili

½ pkg. Mexican beef crumbles

½ cup refried instant beans (prepared)

4 pkg. cream cheese

4 tbsp. jalapeno cheese

1 cup party mix (crushed)

1 cup Jalapeno chips (crushed)

12 pkg. pickled jalapenos

Directions

Halve and dress (remove seeds & veins) Jalapenos and rinse with cool water, set aside.

In a bowl, blend to a nice thickness, chili, beef, jalapeno cheese, jalapeno chips and beans.

Inside the jalapeno halves, run a line of cream cheese, then stuff with the mixture, and top with the party mix.

Enjoy!

Diana's Stuffed Pickles

Contributed by: Diana Kemp

Ingredients

1 pkg. tuna

1 pkg. chili seasoning

2-3 tbsp. pickle juice

¼-2 tbsp. mustard

1 pkg. sweetener

1/3-1/2 a jar of salad dressing

¼ pkg. salsa Verde chips (crushed)

¼ pkg. pork skins (crushed)

¼ pkg. jalapeno chips (crushed)

1 pkg. hot fries (crushed)

4 pkg. pickles (cut in half length wise)

Dash of hot sauce

Cheese puffs (optional)

Directions

In a bowl combine and stir well: tuna, chili seasoning packet, sweetener, two (2) to three (3) tablespoons of pickle juice, one-quarter (1/4) to two (2) tablespoons of mustard, one third (1/3) to one half (1/2) a jar of salad dressing and a dash of hot sauce and set aside for thirty (30) minutes. Scrape the seeds out of the pickle halves; add all four (4) kinds of the crushed chips to the mixture. Spoon the mixture onto the pickle halves.

For a garnish, crush 3 handfuls of cheese puffs and sprinkle on top. Serve any left over mixture with crackers. Makes four to eight servings.

Meals and Snacks

Becca's Faux Chow Chow

Contributed by: Rebecca Martin

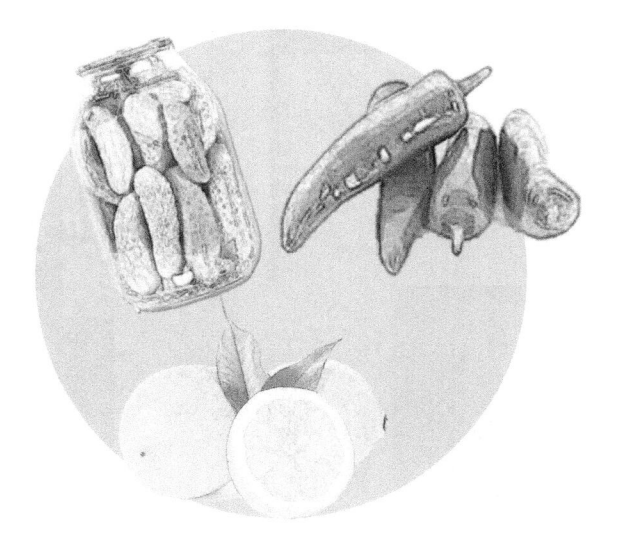

Ingredients

1 pkg. dill pickle (chopped) reserving pickle

1 pkg. jalapeno pepper (chopped)

2 pkg. Lemon or Grape Cool Down

Directions

Pour the pickle juice into a peanut butter jar and stir in the Cool Down. Then add chopped pickle and the jalapeno pepper. Shake well and let stand for a day or two.

Enjoy!

Tuna Noodle Salad

Contributed by: Tanner George Cummings

Ingredients

¼ bag instant rice

1 tuna pouch in water

1 pkg. chicken or chili soup

1 tbsp. salad dressing

¼ pickle (sliced & diced)

1 tbsp. mustard

2 tbsp. jalapeno cheese

½ sleeve saltine crackers

Directions

Crush up the soup (of choice) and put in a bowl, setting seasoning aside. Pour instant rice into the same bowl as the soup is in, adding hot water to cover the soup and rice. Cover and let cook for five (5) minutes. Uncover and drain any excess water from mixture in bowl. Add the soup seasoning packet, tuna pouch, salad dressing, mustard, pickle, and jalapeno cheese. Mix well and enjoy with saltine crackers.

Mock Spam Subway

Contributed by: N.O.

Ingredients

1 loaf of bread

6 pkg. Spam (sliced & diced)

1 pkg. pickle dill regular (sliced & diced)

4 pkg. chili soups (crushed)

Mustard

Squeeze cheese

New large clear trash bags

New small clear trash bags

Strings at least 10 inches long

Small empty chip bag

Directions

Pour the crushed soups and seasoning packets into a large trash bag and add hot water until the soups are covered, then mix well. Tie off and let the soups soak up the hot water.

Completely open a large clear trash bag. Crumble up the entire loaf of bread, add one fourth (1/4) cup of warm water and knead back into dough. Cover and let rise for one (1) hour. In an empty small chip bag pour the Spam into the bag, tie off and put into hot pot to heat up. While the large trash bag is open and flat, flatten out the dough until it is about one fourth (1/4) inches thick, and about seven (7) to nine (9) inches wide and about fifteen (15) to twenty (20) inches long. Drain all excess water juices from the soup and pour the soup evenly across the center of the dough. Pull out the Spam and drain the juices from the Spam and pour on top of the soup. Pour the pickles across the top of the Spam. Put a little bit of the mustard on top of the Spam (to taste). Next add some squeeze cheese (to taste). Carefully and slowly roll from the top evenly lengthwise roll and tuck tightly, slowly peeling away the trash bag. Then roll tightly into the bag until the entire bag is used. Tie a knot on one (1) end about four (4) to five (5) inches; using a string, tie another knot tightly, continue to the end. At the end tie another knot with the bag. Place in water with the heating element and let cook for five (5) hours. Then uncover and enjoy!

Makes two to four servings.

Beef Sloppy Joe

Contributed by: A. Fuentez

Ingredients

1 pkg. Mexican beef crumble

2 tbsp. ketchup

1 pkg. beef seasoning

½ tbsp. onion powder

1 tbsp. BBQ sauce

1 tbsp. pickle juice

1-1/2 tbsp. V8 juice

2 pkg. jalapeno pepper (sliced & diced)

Loaf of bread or crackers

Directions

Put the Mexican beef crumble into the hot pot to heat up.

In a bag, pour in the ketchup, beef seasoning, onion powder, BBQ sauce, pickle juice, V8 juice and the jalapeno peppers and mix well. Drain the grease from the Mexican beef crumble and empty it into a large bowl. Then pour the Sloppy Joe mix in with the crumble and again mix well. Pour contents into another bag, shake and seal and place into a hot pot to heat for one (1) hour. Put some on bread or crackers to enjoy.

Makes two servings.

Meals and Snacks

Ted's Po' Boy BBQ Crunch

Contributed by: Teddy Reed

Ingredients

4 pkg. toasted cheese peanut butter crackers

2 pkg. jalapeno peppers (sliced)

8 tbsp. BBQ sauce (level)

Directions

In a bowl, crumble packs of toasted cheese peanut butter crackers. Next evenly spread the jalapenos over the crackers. Then spread the BBQ sauce over the other layers. Mix all ingredients together well.

Makes one large or two small servings.

Tuna No Soup

Contributed by: Tanner George Cummings

Ingredients

1 pkg. tuna

¼ bag instant refried beans

¼ bag instant rice

¼ bottle salsa

¼ bottle squeeze cheese

2 pkg. jalapeno peppers (sliced)

1 tbsp. salad dressing

Dash of hot sauce (optional)

Directions

Put tuna in the hot pot to heat up for ten (10) to twenty-five (25) minutes. Meanwhile using a large bowl pour in the instant refried beans and instant rice adding enough hot water to barely cover them, cover and set aside to let cook. Uncover and pour in the tuna, salsa, squeeze cheese, jalapeno peppers, and salad dressing and the hot sauce if using, then mix and enjoy!

Meals and Snacks

Sweet N Sour Summer Sausage

Contributed by: Richard Lares

Ingredients

1 bag of pickle juice

2 pkg. beef seasoning

½ tbsp. coffee (instant)

1 bag instant rice (and bag)

1 pkg. orange sports drink

1 pkg. summer sausage (diced)

2 bags pork skins

2 pkg. lemon pies

Directions

Pour and mix the pickle juice, beef seasoning, and coffee, put into a bag and place in hot pot for five (5) minutes. In the rice bag with the rice, add half (1/2) cup of hot water, mix in the sports drink and let set and cook. In a separate bag heat the summer sausage in hot pot. Extract the lemon filling from pies and when the sausage is heated add the filling to the sausage. Add contents of the rice bag evenly into two (2) bowls. Add one bag of crushed pork skins into each bowl. Pour summer sausage mixture evenly into the two (2) bowls. Eat and enjoy!

Makes two servings .

Bentley's Deviled Eggs

Contributed by: Gary Stephens

Ingredients

4 eggs (hard boiled)

1 tbsp. mustard

2 tbsp. salad dressing

1 tbsp. pickle (chopped)

Chili seasoning

Salt

Black pepper

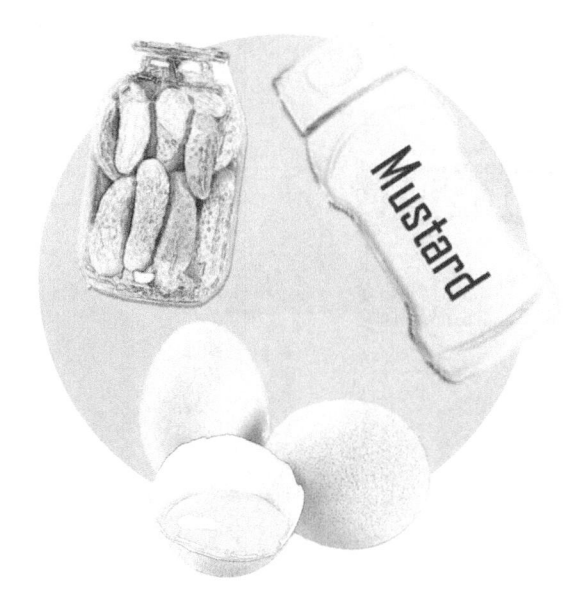

Directions

Carefully remove the shells off of the hard boiled eggs. Cut the eggs in half (1/2), being careful to maintain the egg shape. Remove the yolks and place in a separate bowl. Add the mustard, salad dressing, and pickle to the yolks. Add the salt and pepper to taste.

Scoop the yolk mixture into the void where the yolk was removed. Lightly sprinkle the chili seasoning on top of each egg. Enjoy!

Spameggish Sandwich

Contributed by: Tanner George Cummings

Ingredients

2 eggs (fried)

2 slices bread

1 pkg. jalapeno pepper (sliced)

1 tbsp. sandwich spread

1 tbsp. margarine or butter

1 pkg. Spam

1 tbsp. squeeze cheese

Directions

Spread the margarine or butter on one side of each slice of bread and place on hot surface. Place the Spam on the hot surface and wait a few minutes then flip. On one (1) slice of bread spread the sandwich spread and on the other slice spread the squeeze cheese. Place a fried egg on one (1) slice of toasting bread. Add the jalapeno pepper and the Spam then add the other fried egg and top with the other slice of toasted bread. Enjoy!

Makes one serving.

Breakfast Bowl

Contributed by: Tanner George Cummings

Ingredients

¼ pkg. instant rice

3 pkg. sweetener

1 pkg. trail or energy mix

1 pkg. regular peanuts

1 handful raisins

1 tbsp. margarine or butter

2 tbsp. brown sugar

Directions

Pour the rice in a bowl and pour hot water to top of rice, cover and let rice absorb hot water. Once rice is cooked add the remaining six (6) ingredients, stir and enjoy!

Makes one serving.

Chili Layer

Contributed by: Tanner George Cummings

Ingredients

1 pkg. chili no beans

½ pkg. instant refried beans

1 pkg. flour tortilla

2 pkg. jalapeno peppers (sliced & diced)

Squeeze cheese

Directions

Place chili no beans in a hot pot to heat up. Pour instant refried beans in a bowl and add hot water just to cover the beans. Stir then put on a cover and let them absorb the hot water. In another bowl place down a tortilla, put on a layer of cheese, then a layer of beans, a layer of jalapenos and then pour a layer of chili no beans on top, place down another tortilla and eat with a spoon. Enjoy!

Makes two servings.

Sauces, Sandwich Spreads, Salsa & Dips

Esco's Spread Sauce

Contributed by: Jason Esquivel

Ingredients

1 bottle BBQ sauce

1 bottle hot sauce

1 pkg. pickle (diced & juice reserved)

2 pkg. jalapeno peppers (diced)

2 empty peanut butter jars

Directions

Evenly place the prepared pickle and jalapenos in two (2) peanut butter jars along with the reserved pickle juice. Divide the BBQ sauce and hot sauce evenly in the two (2) jars; stirring well. Use as a dipping sauce with chips or as a condiment. Enjoy!

Sauces, Sandwich Spreads, Salsa & Dips

Paul's Pizza Sauce

Contributed by: Paul Lidji

Ingredients

1 pkg. dill pickle (diced)

2 pkgs. jalapeno peppers (diced)

½ pkg. beef seasoning

¾ tsp. salt

½ tsp. garlic powder

¼ cup pork skins (crushed)

2 tbsp. ketchup

1 tbsp. hot sauce or Habanero sauce

½ tbsp. mustard (for zing)

Directions

Simply combine all ingredients, stir well and enjoy!

Special Sauce

Contributed by: Tanner George Cummings

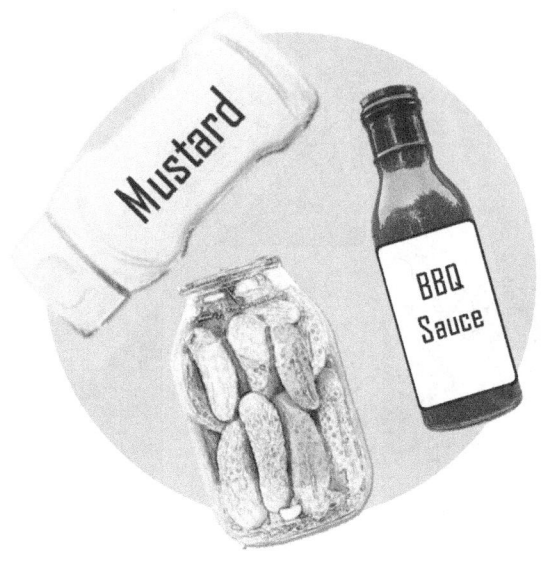

Ingredients

3 tbsp. salad dressing

2-½ tbsp. BBQ sauce

2 tbsp. mustard

1/3 pkg. pickle (sliced & diced)

Directions

Mix all ingredients and enjoy!

Sauces, Sandwich Spreads, Salsa & Dips

Ala Sauce

Contributed by: Tanner George Cummings

Ingredients

2 tbsp. ketchup

1-1/2 tbsp. salad dressing

1-1/2 tbsp. mustard

3 tbsp. barbeque sauce

½ pkg. chili soup seasoning

1/3 pkg. pickle (finely minced)

Directions

In a large bowl mix all ingredients together, then put in a jar and use any way you like.

Homemade Sandwich Spread

Contributed by: Tanner George Cummings

Ingredients

2 tbsp. salad dressing

1 tbsp. sweet pickle relish

1 tbsp. BBQ sauce

½ tbsp. mustard

½ tbsp. ketchup

Directions

Mix all of the ingredients together well. Enjoy!

Dirty's Hot Salsa

Contributed by: Tanner George Cummings

Ingredients

4 tbsp. Habanero hot sauce

3 pkgs. jalapeno peppers (sliced & diced)

1 pkg. regular pickle (sliced & diced)

1/3 cup vinegar or pickle juice (preservative)

1/3 onion flakes or whole onion (sliced & diced)

1 tsp. cayenne pepper

1 Jar

Directions

Mix all ingredients together and pour into the jar. Enjoy!

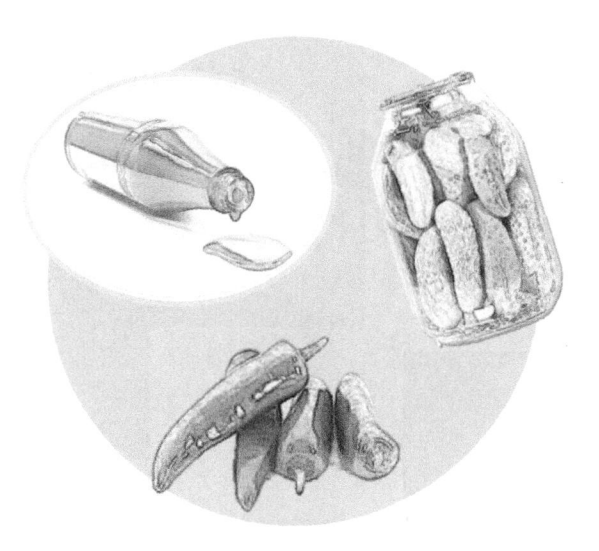

Homemade Salsa

Contributed by: Tanner George Cummings

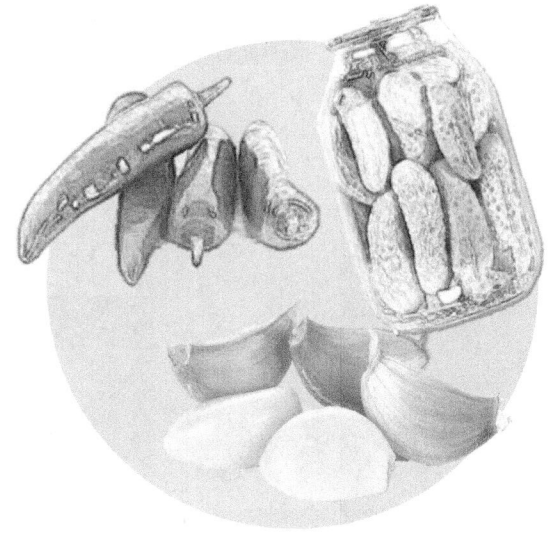

Ingredients

5 pkgs. jalapeno peppers (sliced & diced)

1 whole onion purple/red (sliced & diced)

Pinch of garlic

Pinch of cumin

Pinch of cayenne pepper

Vinegar or pickle juice

Directions

Mix all ingredients and put in a jar and set it in a dark place for several days. Enjoy!

Sauces, Sandwich Spreads, Salsa & Dips

Lori Kay's Holiday Onion Dip

Contributed by: Lori Kay

Ingredients

10 packs cream cheese

1 pack ranch dressing

Season with garlic powder to taste

Season with onion powder to taste

1 tbsp. onion flakes

Directions

Put onion flakes in a cup or bowl add some hot water and allow them to cook for 20 (twenty) to 30 (thirty) minutes. Mix cream cheese in a bowl with just enough ranch dressing to blend into the texture you need. Mix in the garlic and onion powders to your desired taste. Lastly add the cooked onion flakes, mix well.

Makes one small bowl of dip.

Beef-Not-Chor-Chip-Dip

Contributed by: Tanner George Cummings

Ingredients

1 pkg. instant refried beans

1 pkg. Mexican beef crumble

½ bottle squeeze cheese

½ bottle salsa

1 pkg. tortilla chips

Directions

Put an entire package of instant refried beans into a bowl, pour in hot water and mix well until you get a medium thickness; cover and let cook. Put the Mexican beef crumble into hot pot and let heat up for about twenty (20) minutes. Uncover the refried beans and pour in the ½ (half) bottle of squeeze cheese and the ½ (half) bottle of salsa and mix well. Then add the Mexican beef crumble and stir. Open the bag of tortilla chips, dip and enjoy!

Makes enough for two to three people.

Brent's Queso Loco Dip

Contributed by: Brent Neall

Ingredients

½ jar salad dressing

4 pkgs. ranch dressing

2 spoonfuls onion powder

2 spoonfuls garlic powder

2 well rounded spoonfuls of Plantation blend instant coffee

2 pkgs. jalapeno peppers (diced)

1 bottle squeeze cheese (melted)

½ pkg. chili flavored soup seasoning

Black pepper (to taste)

Habanero salsa (to taste)

1 large bowl

Directions

Melt the bottle of squeeze cheese with hot water; pour into the large bowl adding the four (4) packs of ranch dressing also into the bowl. Put in the half (1/2) jar of salad dressing and the diced jalapeno peppers in the bowl; mixing all well. Next add garlic powder, onion powder, chili seasoning and the spoonfuls of coffee and stir. Add the black pepper and Habanero salsa to your taste, stir all well and enjoy!

Sauces, Sandwich Spreads, Salsa & Dips

Summer Sausage Chip Dip

Contributed by: Tanner George Cummings

Ingredients

2 pkgs. summer sausage (sliced & diced)

1 pkg. instant refried beans

½ bottle salsa

½ bottle squeeze cheese

4 pkgs. jalapeno peppers (sliced & diced)

1 bag tortilla chips

Directions

Put the prepared summer sausage into a bag and place into hot pot to heat up. Pour the bag of refried beans into a large bowl and add enough hot water to cover beans, stir and cover then set aside. When the beans are done they should have a medium thickness. Add the salsa, squeeze cheese, jalapeno peppers and stir, cover and place on top of hot pot to keep warm until the summer sausage is ready. When it is heated, pour in the summer sausage mixing well. Open the tortilla chips and dip. Enjoy!

Mistie & Lacey Dip

Contributed by: Mistie Bailey and Lacey Berry

Ingredients

3 pkgs. cream cheese

2 tbsp. pickle juice

1 pkg. chicken soup seasoning

1 pkg. chili soup seasoning

1 pkg. beef soup seasoning

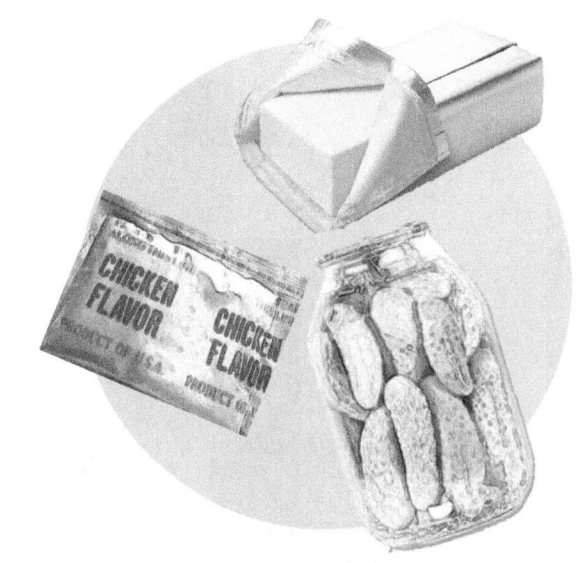

Directions

Put the cream cheese into a bowl or container. Mix in some of each soup seasoning pack (this is done to your own taste). Add pickle juice and mix well. Enjoy with chips or crackers.

Sauces, Sandwich Spreads, Salsa & Dips

Drinks

Pretty Drink

Contributed by: Brent Neall

Ingredients

1 tbsp. coffee (Columbian Reserve)

¼ of a mint/peppermint stick (crushed)

1 pkg. sweetener

1 pkg. cool down (any flavor)

Directions

Combine all of the above ingredients in a coffee mug (12 ounces). Add hot water and stir until the mint stick is dissolved. Drink and enjoy!

Makes one cup.

Sweet Orange Mint Tea

Contributed by: Tanner George Cummings

Ingredients

1 bag of tea

1 pkg. orange cool down or sports energy drink

1 pkg. sweetener

½ peppermint stick (crushed)

Directions

Put tea bag into one coffee mug (12 ounces) of hot water and let steep for three (3) to five (5) minutes; remove tea bag and add remaining ingredients, stir and enjoy!

Makes one cup .

Caffeine Latte

Contributed by: Tanner George Cummings

Ingredients

1 tea bag

1 tbsp. coffee (Columbian Reserve)

½ tbsp. hot chocolate

½ tbsp. powdered milk

1 pkg. sweetener

¼ peppermint stick (crushed)

Directions

Cook the tea bag in a coffee mug (12 ounces) for three (3) to five (5) minutes, remove tea bag and then add remaining ingredients stirring until the peppermint stick is dissolved. Drink and Enjoy!

Makes one cup.

Caffeine - Cino Rush

Contributed by: Tanner George Cummings

Ingredients

1 tea bag

1 tbsp. coffee (Columbian Reserve)

1 pkg. vanilla or French vanilla cappuccino

1 tbsp. hot chocolate

1 tbsp. powered milk

1 pkg. sweetener

¼ peppermint stick (crushed)

Directions

Make tea in a 12 ounce coffee mug, let steep for three (3) to five (5) minutes, remove tea bag and stir in remaining ingredients. Drink and enjoy!

Makes one cup.

Allergy Sootherment

Contributed by: Tanner George Cummings

Ingredients

1 pkg. chicken flavored seasoning

1 tbsp. peanut butter

1 tbsp. powered milk

2 tablets 4 mg. Chlorphen (crushed into powder)

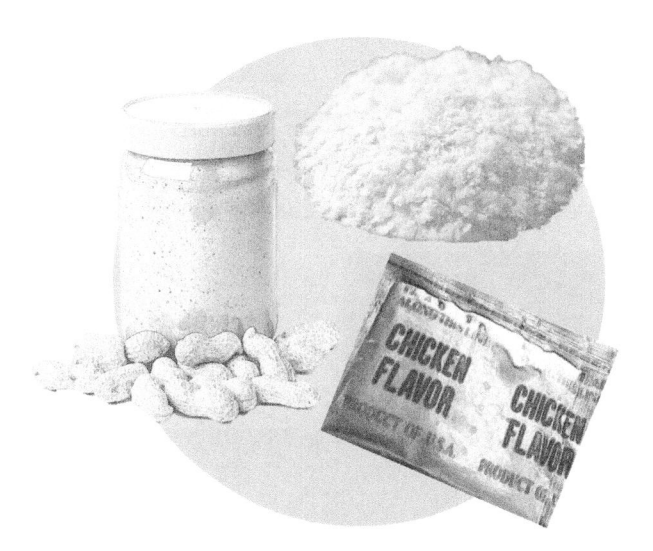

Directions

Put chicken flavored seasoning pack into a cup of hot water, stir then add the peanut butter. Stir and add the powdered milk and the crushed Chlorphen, stir well and drink. Feel better!

Homemade Chocolate Cappuccino

Contributed by: Tanner George Cummings

Ingredients

1 tbsp. instant coffee (Columbian Reserve)

1 tbsp. powdered milk

2 tbsp. hot chocolate

1 pkg. sweetener

Directions

Combine all ingredients into a drinking cup (mug) and add hot water. Stir well and enjoy. Makes one cup (caution one may not be enough they are extremely tasty)

Orange Milky Mint Tea

Contributed by: Tanner George Cummings

Ingredients

1 tea bag

1 pkg. orange sports drink

¼ peppermint stick (crushed)

1 pkg. sweetener

1 tbsp. powered milk

Directions

Put tea bag in a 12 ounce mug with hot water and let it steep for three (3) to five (5) minutes. Remove the bag and add in the other ingredients, stirring well. Drink and enjoy!

Makes one cup.

Chocolate Milk

Contributed by: Tanner George Cummings

Ingredients

1 tbsp. chocolate syrup

¼ cup powdered milk

¼ cup hot chocolate

1 pkg. sweetener

Directions

Pour all ingredients into a quarter (1/4) cup of hot water. Stir until thick, and then keep stirring as you add in cold water. Drink and enjoy!

Makes one cup.

Drinks

Simply Chocolate Milk

Contributed by: Tanner George Cummings

Ingredients

¼ cup powdered milk

2 tbsp. chocolate syrup

Directions

Pour the powdered milk and chocolate syrup into a 12 ounce mug, add cold water and stir until completely dissolved. Drink and enjoy!

Makes one cup.

Peppermint Chocolate Milk

Contributed by: Tanner George Cummings

Ingredients

2 tbsp. hot chocolate

2 tbsp. powdered milk

2 tbsp. chocolate syrup

1-1/2 peppermint sticks (crushed)

Directions

Pour all of the ingredients into a 12 ounce mug or cup. Stir thoroughly as you add in the hot water. Drink carefully with enjoyment!

Makes one cup.

Drinks

Green Hulk Cold Drink

Contributed by: Katy Smith

Ingredients

½ fruit stick (rainbow stick)

1 16 ounce bottle of cold water

½ pkg. sweetener

1 pkg. lime sports energy drink

Directions

Mix all ingredients into the cold bottled water, shake well, drink and enjoy!

Drinks

Mississippi Mudslide

Contributed by: Jonathon Asher

Ingredients

1-1/2 tbsp. coffee (Columbian Reserve)

2 tbsp. hot chocolate

1 pkg. cappuccino (any flavor)

2 pieces fireball candy (crushed)

2 pieces butterscotch candy (crushed)

1 peppermint stick (crushed)

½ tbsp. peanut butter

Directions

Put all the crushed up candy into a cup and add one quarter (1/4) cup of boiling hot water stirring so the candy dissolves. Once the candy is dissolved add in the coffee, stir slowly so the coffee completely dissolves. Next add the hot chocolate and another quarter (1/4) cup of hot water, stir until all is mixed together well. Add the cappuccino and stir again. Finally add the peanut butter and fill the cup with hot water stirring it all together until completely dissolved. Drink carefully and enjoy!

Makes one twelve ounce cup.

Remember Bennigans?

Contributed by: Angela Hamal

Ingredients

1 tsp. Folger coffee (instant)

2 tbsp. cappuccino (Irish crème)

1 tbsp. chocolate syrup

1 pkg. sweetener

Directions

Combine all ingredients into your coffee cup, add hot water, and stir well. Drink and enjoy!

Makes one cup.

Drinks

Butterscotch Cream Coffee

Contributed by: Kathy Smith

Ingredients

1-1/2 tbsp. powdered instant milk

2 pieces butterscotch candy (crushed)

½ tbsp. coffee (instant)

2 pkg. sweetener

Directions

Mix all ingredients in a cup or mug. Pour in hot water and stir until dissolved. Drink and enjoy!

Margaret's Non-Alcoholic Strawberry Margaritas

Contributed by: Margaret Williams

Ingredients

10 pkg. lemon-lime sports drinks

1 bottle water

1 can strawberry soda

Directions

Mix all of the ingredients together, drink and enjoy!

Vanillocolate Coffee

Contributed by: Tanner George Cummings

Ingredients

2 drops vanilla extract

¼ cup instant powdered milk

1 tbsp. instant coffee (Columbian Reserve)

1 tbsp. hot chocolate

½ pkg. French vanilla cappuccino (vanilla will do)

1 pkg. sweetener

Directions

In a cup or mug mix all ingredients with hot water and stir until completely dissolved.

Drink and enjoy!

Health Drink

Contributed by: Tanner George Cummings

Ingredients

1 peppermint stick (crushed)

¼ cup powdered instant milk

1 tbsp. peanut butter

1 pkg. oatmeal (any flavor)

Directions

In a cup or mug combine all ingredients with some hot water to cover ingredients and to cook oatmeal and dissolve the peanut butter and peppermint stick. Let cool and then add cold water to fill cup and enjoy!

Sweet Vanilla Sin Coffee

Contributed by: Tanner George Cummings

Ingredients

1 tbsp. instant coffee (Columbian Reserve)

1 tbsp. instant powdered milk

1 pkg. sweetener

1 drop vanilla extract

1 tsp. brown sugar

Cinnamon (to taste)

Directions

Pour all ingredients into a cup or mug and add hot water, stir well. Sprinkle with cinnamon to your taste Enjoy!

Chocolaty Rich

Contributed by: Tanner George Cummings

Ingredients

2 pkg. Hershey bar (plain)

¼ cup hot chocolate

¼ cup instant powdered milk

Directions

Break up the Hershey bars so that they will fit in the mug or cup, and add the other two ingredients. Add hot water and stir until the candy bar has completely dissolved.

Enjoy!

Sweet Desserts

Banana Nut Cheese Cake

Contributed by: Veronica Henderson

Ingredients

1 pt. banana nut ice cream (melted)

2 pkg. instant powdered milk

1 pkg. macaroon cookies (crushed)

6 pkg. oatmeal pies (mashed)

1 pkg. French vanilla cappuccino

2 pkg. M&M's peanuts (crushed)

Directions

In a bowl crush up the macaroon cookies. Mix up the cappuccino in 8 ounces of hot water, and then mix the two together until it makes dough. Take the mashed oatmeal pies and knead them into the dough. Next knead the crushed M&M's into the dough. Divide the dough into two equal balls. Press one ball flat into the bowl. By now the ice cream should be melted. In a separate bowl, mix the ice cream and powdered milk together until nice and thick. Pour two-thirds (2/3) of the ice cream mixture on top of the flattened dough. Then flatten down the second ball of dough and lay it on top of the ice cream mixture. Top off the dough with the remaining third of the ice cream mixture. Let stand covered for at least four (4) hours. Enjoy!

Sweet Desserts

Strawberry Cheesecake

Contributed by: Erica Anthony

Ingredients

1 pt. strawberry ice cream (melted)

2 pkg. cream cheese

5 pkg. banana Moon pies

1 pkg. instant milk powder

1 pkg. Snickers bars

¾ pkg. duplex cookies (crushed including crème filling)

2 pkg. oatmeal pies (crumbled)

5 tbsp. water

Directions

Combine melted ice cream and cream cheese and mix well. Add powdered milk and stir until thick. Melt Snickers and banana Moon pies in a hot pot, and then stir into the ice cream mixture.

In a separate bowl mix the crushed cookies and the crumbled oatmeal pies. Add the water gradually until you can mold the mixture into a crust inside the bowl. Add the ice cream mixture, and let sit for at least four (4) hours.

Makes four to eight servings.

Ice Cream Cheesecake

Contributed by: Quintasha Harris

Ingredients

Crust

1 pkg. cookie of the week (crushed)

1 pkg. brown sugar oatmeal

5 tbsp. water (add more or use less for desired texture)

Filling

1 pint ice cream (melted) your flavor choice

2 pkg. instant powered milk

1 candy bar (melted) your flavor choice

1 pkg. cream cheese

Directions

Place crushed cookies and brown sugar oatmeal into a bowl, add water, mix thoroughly and mold into a separate bowl. (This is the crust).

Slowly add the instant powdered milk to the melted ice cream stirring until smooth an thick. (Do not add any water to this filling!) Pour the filling into the crust and let stand uncovered for one (1) hour. Next place melted candy bar and cream cheese into a small chip bag and mix well. Tear off a corner of the bag and decorate the cheesecake, Enjoy!

Sweet Desserts

Liv's Lemon Cheesecake

Contributed by: Clifford Livingston

Ingredients

3 pkg. powdered instant milk

3 pkg. cream cheese

2 pkg. lemon cool downs

1 pkg. vanilla crème cookies

6 fl. oz. Sprite or water

Directions

For the crust: separate cookies from the crème fillings into two bowls. Use hot pot insert to crush the cookies into a fine crumbs. Add one (1) lemon cool down to the cookie crumbs and mix well. Put three spoons of crumbs into the empty cookie tray for use later. Add six (6) spoons of Sprite or water to the crumbs and mix well, until doughy. Form dough into a ball; flatten the dough into the bottom and up the sides of the bowl.

For the filling: add three (3) pkg. of cream cheese and the other lemon cool down to the bowl with the crème filling from cookies. Mix well until smooth with no lumps. Add one (1) pkg. of instant powdered milk to the filling mixing until dry and crumbly. Repeat this process until you have added all three (3) pkg. Next pour in three (3) ounces of Sprite or water into the filling and stir until creamy. Then add the last three (3) ounces of Sprite or water and continue stirring for at least five (5) minutes but no longer than ten (10) minutes. Pour the filling into the crust and sprinkle the reserved cookies crumbs over the top. Allow to set covered for six (6) hours or overnight. Enjoy!

Sweet Desserts

Liv's Apple Cinnamon Cheesecake

Contributed by: Clifford Livingston

Ingredients

3 pkg. instant powdered milk

3 pkg. cream cheese

1 pkg. lemon cool down

1 pkg. vanilla crème cookies

7 fl. oz Sprite or water

1 pkg. apple cinnamon oatmeal

Directions

For the crust: start by pouring the oatmeal into one of the bowls. Separate the oatmeal, sugar- cinnamon, and apple pieces. Put the apples pieces into a cup and add about one (1) fl. ounce of Sprite or water to the apples and let sit. Put the oatmeal into a bowl and set aside. Leave cinnamon-sugar in the bowl and set aside. Now take the cookies and separate the cream filling from the cookies. Put the cream filling in the bowl with the sugar-cinnamon. Put the cookies into the bowl with the oatmeal. Use the hot pot insert to crush cookies into fine crumbs. Add half a packet of the lemon cool down into the cookie crumbs and mix well. Spoon out three (3) spoons of the crumbs into the empty cookie package for later use. Add six (6) spoons of Sprite or water to crumb mixture in the bowl. Blend the liquid with the crumbs until doughy. Form the dough into a ball. Now press the dough into the bottom and halfway up the sides of the bowl.

For the filling: add the cream cheese and the rest of the packet of lemon cool down to the bowl with the sugar-cinnamon and cookie crème filling. Mix well. Add one (1) pkg. of the instant milk to the mixture and stir until crumbly. Repeat until all three (3) milk pkg. are mixed in. Pour off the liquid from the soaking apples into the filling mixture. Pour three (3) ounces of Sprite or water into the filling and mix. Add another three ounces and stir for at least five (5) minutes, but no longer then ten (10) minutes. Pour the filling into the crust and arrange the apple bits on top of the filling. Sprinkle the reserved cookie crumbs over the top. Allow to set for about six (6) hours or overnight. Enjoy!

Sweet Desserts

Liv's Strawberry Ice Cream Cheesecake

Contributed by: Clifford Livingston

Ingredients

3 pkg. instant powdered milk

3 pkg. cream cheese

6 fluid ounces Sprite, strawberry soda or water

6 tbsp. water

1 pkg. vanilla crème cookies

½ pint strawberry ice cream or ½ bottle strawberry jam

1 pkg. lemon cool down

Directions

Set the pint of ice cream on top of the hot pot to melt, but not completely, as you will only use half (1/2).

For the crust: separate the cookies from the crème fillings into two bowls. Using the hot pot insert crush the cookies into a fine crumb. Add half (1/2) of the cool down into the cookie crumbs and stir together. Take three (3) spoons of crumbs and put them in the empty cookie tray for later use. Add 6 spoons of Sprite or water to the bowl of crumbs and mix well, forming the dough into a ball. Press the ball of dough flat into the bottom and halfway up the sides of the bowl.

For the filling: add the three packets of cream cheese and the other half (1/2) of the cool down to the bowl of crème filling from cookies. Mix well until there are no lumps. Add one (1) pouch of the milk to the mixture and stir until dry and crumbly. Repeat the process with remaining two (2) milk pouches. Pour in three (3) fluid ounces of Sprite or water and stir until creamy. Pour in the half (1/2) pint of strawberry ice cream (or strawberry jam if using instead of ice cream) and blend lightly. Pour in the remaining Sprite or water and mix until all the lumps are gone. Blend for at least five (5) minutes but no more then ten (10) minutes. Pour the filling into the crust and sprinkle with the cookie crumbs saved in cookie tray over the top. Allow to set for about six (6) hours or over night. Enjoy! Makes one to eight servings.

Sweet Desserts

Liv's Chocolate Cheesecake

Contributed by: Clifford Livingston

Ingredients

3 pkg. instant powdered milk

3 pkg. cream cheese

1 pkg. Three Musketeers or two Hershey's bars

¾ cup hot chocolate

6 spoons of water

1 pkg. Duplex/double fudge crème cookies

1 pkg. lemon cool down

6 fluid ounces of Sprite or water

Directions

Put chocolate bars into a water proof bag (clean chip or plastic etc.) and melt in hot pot.

For the crust: separate crème filling from the cookies into two bowls. Use hot pot insert to crush the cookies into fine crumbs. Add half (1/2) of the lemon cool down and one quarter (1/4) cup of the hot chocolate into cookie crumbs, mix well. Put three (3) spoons of crumb mixture aside on empty cookie tray to use later. Add six (6) spoons of water to the bowl of crumbs and mix into dough. Form the dough into a ball. Press the dough flat into the bottom and halfway up the sides of the bowl.

For the filling: add the three (3) cream cheese packets, the other half (1/2) of the lemon cool down, the melted chocolate and the one half (1/2) cup of hot chocolate to the bowl of cookie crème filling. Mix well, until there are no lumps. Add one (1) pkg. milk to mixture and stir until dry and crumbly. Repeat the process with the remaining two (2) pkgs. of milk. Pour three (3) spoons of Sprite or water into filling and stir well. Add the remaining three (3) spoons of Sprite or water into the filling and stir until no lumps. Stir for five (5) minutes, but no longer than ten (10) minutes. Pour the filling into the crust and sprinkle the saved cookie crumbs on top. Allow to set for six (6) hours or overnight. Enjoy!

Sweet Desserts

Loving Lemon Meringue Pie

Contributed by: Shonda Loving

Ingredients

20 cream cheese pouches

1 bag powdered milk

½ pkg. vanilla wafers or ½ pkg. vanilla crème cookies

2 pkg. lemon sports drink

Water

Directions

Using two separate bowls separate the crème filling from the cookies. Next crush up the bowl of cookies until very fine and dampen them lightly with water making sure to add a little of the sports drink for lemon flavor, and press it into a crust in the bowl.

In the bowl with the crème filling add all the cream cheese, milk and sports drink, adding water when necessary. Stir until desired thickness and then pour into the crust. Let set for about fifteen (15) or twenty (20) minutes until ready to eat.

Enjoy!

Wild Bill's Cream Cheese Spread

Contributed by: William Vehon

Ingredients

1 pkg. duplex crème cookies

½ pkg. regal graham cookies

15 pkg. cream cheese

1/3 cup instant powered milk

1/3 cup hot chocolate

1/3 cup water

Directions

Split duplex crème cookies into halves and set aside in a bowl. In a separate bowl mix the cream cheese, powered milk, hot chocolate and water, stirring into a smooth batter. Crush up the graham cookies into little chunks and sprinkle over the batter and then mix in thoroughly.

Spread one half (1/2) spoonfuls onto the top of the separated duplex cookie halves.

Enjoy!

Fruddy's Banana Pudding

Contributed by: Pamela Harris

Ingredients

2 pints banana pudding ice cream

1 pkg. instant powered milk

1 pkg. vanilla wafers

Sweet Desserts

Directions

Let ice cream melt. Add half (1/2) pkg. of the powdered milk to each pint of ice cream and then mix all together in a large spread bowl. Using another spread bowl, line it with the vanilla wafers. Pour some of the melted ice cream mixture on top of the vanilla wafers and then add another layer of vanilla wafers then add another layer of the ice cream mixture, then a layer of vanilla wafers, and another layer of ice cream mixture, repeating process until everything is used. Let stand covered for one (1) hour.

Enjoy!

Margaret's Creole Banana Pudding

Contributed by: Margaret Williams

Ingredients

1 pint banana pudding ice cream (melted)

1 pkg. instant powered milk

½ cup of slightly crushed vanilla wafers

7 whole vanilla wafers

Directions

In a spread bowl, mix the powered milk and the melted ice cream together. Next, while stirring, pour in the crushed vanilla wafers. After they are added garnish the edges with the 7 whole wafers.

Makes two servings.

Cherry's Banana Pudding

Contributed by: Cheryl Haga

Ingredients

1 pint banana nut or banana split ice cream (melted)

5 pkg. banana Moon pies

1 bag vanilla wafers

Directions

In a large spread bowl, break up a Moon pie and make this into a layer. Spread some of the melted ice cream on top and then add a layer of vanilla wafers. Repeat the process until all the Moon pies and ice cream are used up. Let the pudding sit covered for one (1) hour.

Enjoy!

Diana's Banana Pudding

Contributed by: Diana Kemp

Ingredients

3 pkg. banana Moon pies

1 pkg. vanilla wafers

1 pkg. energizer mix (crushed) optional

Butter/margarine

Directions

Mash up the Moon pies, add some butter/ margarine and melt in a hot pot insert, to form a pudding.

In a large spread bowl, arrange a layer of vanilla wafers, cover with some of the pudding, and then another layer of vanilla wafers. Cover with another layer of the pudding, then another layer of vanilla wafers. Repeat with the pudding until all the pudding is gone.

Add the energizer mix on one of the layers or on the top (if using). Let the pudding set up for thirty (30) minutes to one (1) hour.

Eat and enjoy!

Makes one to two servings.

J.C's Lemon Pudding

Contributed by: James Carlberg

Ingredients

1 bag vanilla wafers

1 bag instant powered milk

1 pkg. lemon cool down

1 pkg. sweetener

1 can Sprite

Directions

Crush half (1/2) the vanilla wafers in a spread bowl, and set aside the other half (1/2). Pour the powered milk, sweetener and the lemon cool down into the crushed vanilla wafers in the spread bowl. (Pour them in when they are dry; not while wet). Slowly pour in about three quarters (3/4) of the sprite into the dry ingredients and stir until the mixture is thick like a pudding texture. Spread a thin layer of the mixture into another spread bowl and then begin stacking layers of the whole reserved vanilla wafers over the layers of pudding mixture. Repeat this layering process until all ingredients are used.

Eat and enjoy!

Granola Bars

Contributed by: Wallace Clark

Ingredients

4 pkg. maple brown sugar or apple cinnamon oatmeal

2 pkg. trail mix

2 pkg. vanilla Moon pies

3 pkg. Nutty Buddy bars

15 pieces butterscotch disks

1 pkg. Multi-grain caramel chips

1 lg. empty chip bag

1 lg. bowl

Directions

Open both Moon pies and remove the marshmallow filling. Place filling into a hot pot insert along with the fifteen (15) butterscotch disks, add about five (5) tbsp. of hot water into the insert cup. Set into hot pot and let cook until butterscotch candy and marshmallow are completely melted. Crush both the nutty bars and multi-grain chips. Place into a large bowl along with four (4) pkg. of oatmeal. Crush up the trail mix into small pieces and place into the bowl. Mix well. Remove insert from hot pot (carefully it is hot!) and slowly pour over contents in the bowl. With clean hands, mash contents into a square. Cut with a spoon into two inch by three inch portions.

Allow to cool and enjoy!

Sweet Desserts

Sweet Granola Pie

Contributed by: Tanner George Cummings

Ingredients

2 pkg. vanilla crème cookies

4 pkg. instant oatmeal plain

2 pkg. sweetener

1 pkg. unsalted peanuts (chopped- if salted wash and then chop)

1 pkg. trail mix

1 pkg. multi-grain caramel chips

1 cup instant powdered milk

1 lg. bowl

1 empty bag for icing

Directions

Separate the crème from both pkg. of cookies into the empty bag, set aside. Crush one pkg. cookies and place in the bowl adding approximately four (4) tbsp. of lukewarm water and knead into a dough, then flatten it into the bottom of the bowl. Crush up the peanuts, trail mix, multi-grain chips, and the four (4) pkg. of plain oatmeal and add three (3) tbsp. water, knead into dough and pour on top of the bottom crust and flatten out evenly. Take the other pkg. of cookies and repeating the instructions for the bottom crust, make, and then place on top and flatten out evenly.

Icing: using the bag with the crème filling that was set aside, add one-third (1/3) cup of the powered milk and add two (2) tbsp. of warm water (adding more until desired thickness for icing). Mix up well, cut the corners of the bag and pour on top, spreading it out evenly.

Makes eight servings.

Charlie's Butterscotch Brownies

Contributed by: Mistie Bailey

Ingredients

1 pkg. vanilla wafers or double fudge cookies

1 pkg. butterscotch candies

2-3 cups of hot chocolate (depending on how rich you want it)

Directions

Crush all the cookies in a bowl. In a separate container crush the candies. Take half (1/2) of the candy and mix with the crushed cookies. Mix in one and a half (1-1/2) to two and a half (2-1/2) cups of the hot chocolate to the mixture (according to how rich) slowly add hot water until doughy. Put the remaining half (1/2) cup candy and hot chocolate in a cup and add a little bit of hot water. Stir mixture into a glaze. Press the dough mixture flat into the bowl and pour the glaze over it.

Sweet Desserts

Mock Brownies

Contributed by: M. Wells

Ingredients

½ cup hot chocolate

1 pkg. chocolate or duplex crème cookies

1 pkg. unsalted peanuts (chopped and crushed)

½ cup powdered milk

2 pkg. sweetener

Directions

First separate the crème from the cookies and set aside. Put the cookies in a bowl and crush into a fine powder, add in the half (1/2) cup of powdered milk and the half (1/2) cup of hot chocolate with one quarter (1/4) of lukewarm water and begin to knead into a dough. Sprinkle in the two (2) sweeteners and then knead some more. Using an empty chip bag, or some type of covered surface flatten out (the thickness, width and length will determine your brownie count.) Sprinkle the peanuts on top. If using the crème icing add one (1) tsp. water and mix well and pour over the top of the brownies. Cut and enjoy!

Sweet Desserts

Mud Pie Brownies

Contributed by: Sherri Whimmer

Ingredients

2 lg. tbsp. peanut butter

Full cup hot chocolate

1 sleeve Graham crackers or vanilla wafers

Directions

Fill an empty peanut butter jar or hot pot insert almost to the top with hot chocolate, add a little bit of water and stir until gooey. (Careful too much water will make it runny) so a little at a time. Add the two (2) large tablespoons of peanut butter and stir until peanut butter blends with the gooey chocolate; place into hot pot for ten (10) to twenty (20) minutes. In a bowl crush one sleeve of Graham crackers or a half (1/2) bag of vanilla wafers, crush until very fine. Pour the peanut butter and chocolate mixture over the crushed cookies mixing well and add water if needed. Cover and let set for one (1) hour.

Enjoy!

Rich Peanut Butter Brownies

Contributed by: Tanner George Cummings

Ingredients

4- 1/2 jars peanut butter (1- 5 pound can of peanut butter)

1 bag brownie mix

½ pkg. oatmeal plain (small brown paper bag)

Directions

In a foot tub or on a flat covered surface pour the brownie mix with two (2) and a half (1/2) cups of water and knead like dough with the peanut butter. Keep kneading until the brownie mix and peanut butter sticks to itself. Add in the half (1/2) bag of oatmeal and knead until all of the oatmeal and the brownie peanut butter mix are thoroughly mixed together.

Makes about eighteen three inch by five inch by one inch thick brownies.

Sweet Desserts

Fudge Cookie Sandwiches with Butterscotch Icing

Contributed by: Adam Worster & Brian Blackburn

Ingredients

1 pkg. duplex/vanilla crème cookies

1 pkg. chocolate chip macaroon cookies

¾ cup hot chocolate

1 pkg. instant powdered milk

13-15 pieces butterscotch candy

1 stick Chick-o-stick (crushed)

2 pkg. sweetener

Directions

Icing: Crush butterscotch candy and place into a cup. Cover candy with the hot water and stir to dissolve (careful not too much water.) Separate the crème filling from the cookies putting the crème filling in a bowl add the dissolved butterscotch, powdered milk, and sweetener. If needed add a little more milk if there is too much water on the butterscotch, stirring well.

Fudge: Crush the cookies in a bowl and add the hot chocolate. Mixing together with seven (7) or eight (8) tablespoons of water, being careful not to add too much water. Mix fudge until it sticks to itself. Separate fudge into sixteen (16) equal portions and sandwich them to chocolate chip macaroons or vanilla crème cookies or both. Add icing on top of the cookie sandwiches. Crush chick-o-stick and sprinkle on top of the icing. Enjoy!

Peanut Butter Fudge Bar with Peppermint Icing

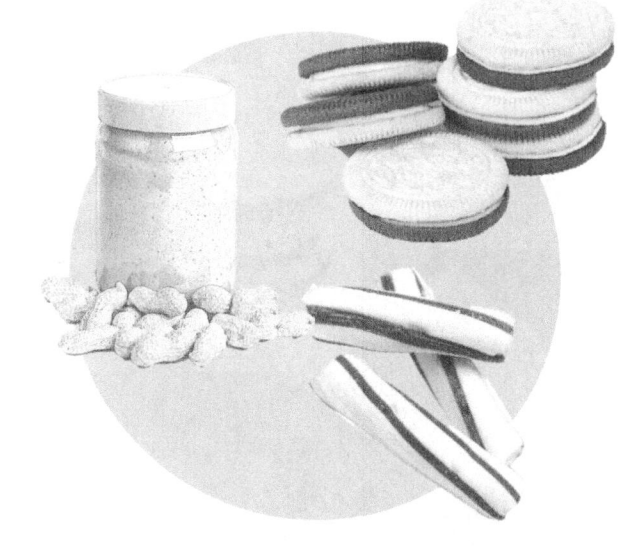

Contributed by: Michael Brown

Ingredients

1 pkg. Vanilla/Duplex cookies (save cookie trays)

2 sticks peppermint sticks (crushed)

4 pkg. plain oatmeal

1 full cup hot chocolate

3 lg. tbsp. peanut butter

Directions

Icing: Separate crème from cookies and place into hot pot insert. Add the crushed peppermint sticks and three (3) tbsp. of hot water. Stir and place into hot pot until it is dissolved and blended together.

Bars: Pour hot chocolate into a cup and add hot water as you stir. Hot water should be no more than approximately six (6) tablespoons. Stir until thick and smooth then add in the oatmeal and peanut butter and stir well. Next crush the cookies adding a little hot water, then add the peanut butter fudge mixture, and mix until it is thick and sticks together.

Place portions of the peanut butter mixture into cookie trays and flatten out. Pour the icing on top.

Enjoy!

Nutty Chocolate Pies with Peanut Butter Icing

Contributed by: Tanner George Cummings

Ingredients

2 tbsp. peanut butter

1 pkg. vanilla/duplex crème cookies

1 cup hot chocolate

½ cup instant powdered milk

4 pkg. peanuts (chopped)

¾ cup chocolate syrup

Directions

Icing: Separate the crème from the cookies and put into the hot pot insert with the peanut butter and five (5) tbsp. of hot water and stir until smooth and creamy. Place into hot pot to keep warm.

Pie crust: Take the cookies and crush them up and add a little warm water so you can knead it into dough. If too watery add powdered milk and continue to knead until doughy. Then flatten down in a large bowl making it even, next pour the chocolate syrup on top. Now pour the icing over the top then finish with the chopped peanuts sprinkled on top. Let it set for thirty (30) to forty-five (45) minutes. Cut into four to eight pieces and enjoy!

Chocolatey Peanut Butter Bars

Contributed by: Medina

Ingredients

¼ pkg. vanilla crème cookies

1 cup hot chocolate

¼ pkg. vanilla wafers

1 tbsp. peanut butter (heaping)

1 cup powdered instant milk

3 pkg. sweetener

Empty cookie tray

Directions

Separate the crème from the vanilla cookies into a cup and set aside. In a large bowl put the wafers, hot chocolate, peanut butter and the vanilla cookies adding one spoonful of hot water and begin to knead into dough. Divide the dough into three (3) even balls and smash into empty cookie tray evenly. Pour the sweetener and powdered milk into the cup with reserved crème filling adding two (2) tbsp. of hot water and stir until it is a smooth thick crème. Then layer the top of all three (3) bars with the crème. Enjoy!

Chocolate Vanilla Wafer Bars

Contributed by: Billie D. Collins

Ingredients

1 pkg. vanilla wafers (crushed)

1 cup hot chocolate

½ pkg. m&m's candy (crushed)

1 cup instant powdered milk

2 empty cookie trays

1 large bowl

Directions

Crush up the vanilla wafers into a fine powder then pour into the large bowl adding in the hot chocolate, powdered milk, and m&m's. Add one cup lukewarm water and begin to knead into dough. The dough should be nice and thick in consistency. Make six even balls and smash one down evenly in each row.

Makes six bars.

Dream Bar Cake

Contributed by: Billy Black

Ingredients

2 pkg. vanilla crème cookies

2 pkg. cream cheese

3 pkg. orange sports drink or six (6) orange cool downs

1 bag orange slices (optional)

Directions

Separate the crème from the cookies and place in a cup adding the cream cheese. In a separate cup place either the orange drink or the cool downs filling up the cup halfway with hot water, stir well until the drink powder is completely dissolved. Top off with cold water than set aside. In a commissary bowl crush the cookies into a fine powder, than add three (3) to four (4) commissary spoons of the dissolved orange drink. Knead until dough is formed; press into the bottom of the bowl. Next add a few spoonfuls of the orange drink to the crème/ cream cheese mixture and blend into an icing. After mixing smooth spread on top of the cookie dough and cut into pieces.

You can now place an orange slice on each piece or using a handful of crushed orange candies (from bag of penny candy) spread over the cake.

Sweet Desserts

Snickers Cake

Contributed by: Mattie McGinnis

Ingredients

4 bars Snickers

1 pkg. vanilla crème cookies

4 pkg. cream cheese

Directions

Mix Snickers, cream cheese and the crème from the cookies in the insert from the hot pot. Add half (1/2) cup of water and place into hot pot and let melt. Crush the cookies for a crust. Adding a quarter (1/4) cup of water, knead into dough and then shape into the bottom of the bowl. Pour the melted ingredients onto the crust and let set, as it cools down it will harden. Enjoy!

Sweet Desserts

Luscious Lava Nut Cake

Contributed by: Kathy Smith

Ingredients

1 pkg. vanilla crème cookies

2 pkg. Snickers candy bars

1 pkg. Milky Way candy bars

1 pkg. regular peanuts

Directions

Remove the crème filling from the cookies. Crush the cookies and add water (if needed) until you have a cookie crust. Crush the peanuts and then mix them into the cookie dough. Roll out the cookie dough into a pizza form. Put the Snickers and Milky Way bars on top and roll them inside the dough. Place the cake into an empty chip bag or the hot pot insert cup and cook the cake in the hot pot for ten (10) to fifteen (15) minutes.

Then flatten down in a large bowl and cut into eight pieces. Enjoy by yourself or share!

Sweet Desserts

Mickey's Peanut Butter Oatmeal

Contributed by: Valerie Santilanez

Ingredients

¾ cup instant powdered milk

1-1/2 pkg. oatmeal (regular flavor)

3 tbsp. peanut butter (melted)

1 pkg. sweetener

½ bar Butterfinger candy (crunched)

Directions

Cook oatmeal with hot water making it thick. Pour into a cup and add powdered milk. Melt the peanut butter and add to the oatmeal. Stir in the one (1) sweetener and add the crunched Butterfinger on the top of the light milky peanut butter oatmeal and enjoy!

Sweet Desserts

Oooie-Gooey Chewies

Contributed by: Cheryl Haga

Ingredients

10 sticks Chic-o-stick

3 bars Milky Way candy (melted)

1 bag Butterfingers cookies (crushed)

1 empty chip bag

Directions

Crush Chic-o-sticks and cookies in a large bowl. Melt the candy bars in the hot pot insert in the hot pot. Pour the melted candy bars into the bowl with the crushed chic-o-sticks and crushed Butterfingers cookies mixing well. Place one half (1/2) spoonful scoop on flattened chip bag. Let sit for one (1) hour then enjoy!

Sweet Desserts

Sherry's Chocolate Almond Cherry Pie Delight

Contributed by: Sherry Johnson

Ingredients

1 pkg. vanilla crème cookies

2 pkg. cherry pies

2 pkg. Snickers (almond)

½ cup instant powdered milk

1 pkg. vanilla cappuccino (instant)

Directions

Put cherry pies and Snickers into an empty coffee bag and heat for one (1) hour. Take cookies apart, set aside the plastic tray, scrape icing into a cup and save. In a bowl crush the cookies; using some hot water and half (1/2) of the powdered milk and half (1/2) of the cappuccino; mix all together with a spoon until you have a thick mixture. Put into the plastic cookie tray and spread evenly throughout the three sections. Pour melted Snickers and cherry pies evenly over the three sections of the cookie tray. Stir rest of milk powder and cappuccino into the saved cup of filling and mix until it is thick. Spread out evenly over each of the three sections, cover and let stand over night.

No Bake Cookies

Contributed by: Tanner George Cummings

Ingredients

½-1 cup peanut butter

1-2 pkg. oatmeal (any flavor)

½ cup hot chocolate

Directions

Mix all ingredients together. Spread out on an open chip bag into approximately twelve inch by eight inch square.

Makes two dozen two inch square cookies.

Becca's Peanut Butter Oatey Oatmeal

Contributed by: Rebecca Martin

Ingredients

1 pkg. instant oatmeal

2 pkg. oatmeal crème pies

1 tbsp. peanut butter

Directions

Pour oatmeal into a bowl, add hot water and stir well. Mix in the peanut butter until blended. Break up the oatmeal crème pies, add and mix well. Enjoy!

Sweet Desserts

Orange-Lemon or Chocolate Kolaches

Contributed by: Merri Joy Lettining

Ingredients

4 pkg. honey buns

1 pkg. instant powdered milk

2 pkg. orange or lemon sports drink or 2 heaping spoonfuls of hot chocolate

Directions

Press down center rings of the honey buns with a spoon. Place milk and sports drink in a bowl (or the hot chocolate) add small amounts of water and stir until you get a semi thick consistency. It should be similar to a cheesecake filling before it sets up. Then spoon the mixture into the center of the honey buns and let sit for several hours.

Serves four.

Banana Smoores

Contributed by: Tanner George Cummings

Ingredients

1 sleeve Honey Graham crackers

3 pkg. banana pies

2 bars Hershey's plain (melted)

Directions

Separate the crust from the banana pies and place marshmallow half on top of a graham cracker. Take a portion of the melted chocolate and place on a graham cracker and sandwich with the graham cracker with the marshmallow and enjoy!

Armadillo Eggs

Contributed by: Flint Kerby

Ingredients

½ cup cocoa (hot chocolate)

2 tbsp. peanut butter (heaping)

7 chocolate chip cookies (crushed)

1 pkg. m&m's (finely crushed)

5 vanilla wafers (finely crushed)

Several tbsp. of water

Directions

Mix all ingredients (except crushed vanilla wafers) together until the mixture no longer sticks to the bowl. Take the mixture and roll into quarter size balls. Roll the quarter sized balls into the finely crushed vanilla wafer dust. Enjoy!

Sweet Desserts

Strawberry Vanilla Chocolate Mamas

Contributed by: Cox

Ingredients

1 pkg. chocolate chip cookies

1 pkg. cereal

1 pkg. hot chocolate

1 pkg. crème cookies (vanilla or duplex)

1 jar strawberry preserves jelly

1 pkg. instant powdered milk

1 pkg. powdered sugar (optional)

Directions

Pour half (1/2) of the bag of hot chocolate and half (1/2) of the powdered milk into a large bowl, add a little bit of water and knead together until nice and thick.

In an empty bag crush up some cereal and mix it into the chocolate mixture. In another bowl separate the crème from the cookies (setting cookie shells aside) and pour some strawberry jelly in and stir until the two ingredients become one (1). In another bowl, put some chocolate chip cookies down flat and place a spoonful of the chocolate mixture on top of each chocolate cookie. Then place a cookie shell from set aside cookies on top of the chocolate mixture. Next, on top of that cookie put some of the strawberry mixture. Finally sprinkle powdered sugar on top of each cookie. Then repeat until all of the chocolate chip cookies are gone or the chocolate mixture is used up.

Enjoy!

Sweet Desserts

Raspberry Flavored Tootsie Pop Icing

Contributed by: Tanner George Cummings

Ingredients

1 pkg. Powdered Instant milk

¼ pkg. hot chocolate

½ tbsp. red Kool Ade

Directions

Pour all ingredients into a bowl and three (3) tbsp. hot water and stir.

You may want to add more or less water depending on the thickness and texture that you desire.

Sweet Desserts

Tippy's Coffee Balls

Contributed by: Kristen Metz

Ingredients

1 pkg. vanilla or double fudge Duplex cookies

1 tbsp. instant coffee (heaping)

2 tbsp. hot chocolate (heaping)

Directions

Scrape the crème filling out of the cookies into a hot pot insert. Place insert with filling into hot pot to melt. Crush cookies in a bowl. Grind coffee into a fine powder and add powdered coffee to the crushed cookies. Add a little water until the mixture is moist, but not wet. Roll mixture into little balls. Pour melted crème into the upside down hot pot lid and roll the coffee balls in it. Then roll them in the chocolate.

Makes about fifteen balls depending on the size you roll.

Holiday Fruity Fruit

Contributed by: Mattie McGinnis

Ingredients

2 oranges (whole)

2 apples (whole)

2 fruit sticks

2 orange sports drink packs (or any flavor)

1 handful sunflower seeds

Directions

Cut oranges and apples into small pieces. Finely crush fruit sticks. Place the oranges, apples, fruit sticks, sports drinks and sunflower seeds into a bowl. Toss ingredients together and let marinate for a few minutes.

Serve and enjoy!

Extra Sweet Honey Buns

Contributed by: Tanner George Cummings

Ingredients

1 pkg. Honey bun

1 bar Three Musketeers or Snickers

1 tbsp. peanut butter

1-1/2 tbsp. chocolate syrup

Directions

Heat up the honey bun. Melt the candy bar of choice on the top of the heated honey bun. Melt the peanut butter and pour over the top. Heat up the chocolate syrup and pour on top. Cut in half, serves two people.

Sweet Desserts

Tippy's Tipperroo

Contributed by: Kristin Metz

Ingredients

1 pkg. vanilla Moon Pie

2 bars Hershey's plain bar

2 pkg. peanuts, salted (chopped)

Directions

Take the two Hershey bars and melt them in hot pot inset in the hot pot. Place Moon pies in the middle of a large bowl and pour the melted Hershey bar all over the Moon pie until it is completely covered. Take the chopped peanuts and sprinkle over the top, let set for one (1) hour. Enjoy!

Sweet Desserts

Fried Peanut Butter & Jelly Sandwich

Contributed by: Tanner George Cummings

Ingredients

2 tbsp. butter or margarine

2 slices bread

2 tbsp. peanut butter

2 tbsp jelly (grape or strawberry)

Directions

Place the margarine or butter on one (1) side of each slice of bread and place on a hot surface. Then on one (1) slice of bread put the peanut butter and on the other put the jelly. After heating both slices flip the jelly bread on top of the peanut butter one and remove from the hot surface. Carefully eat because ingredients are hot and delicious!

In-between Snacks

Contributed by: Tanner George Cummings

Ingredients

1 pkg. any flavor soup (crushed)

1 handful Party mix (crushed)

1 handful corn chips (crushed)

1 handful cheese curls (crushed)

Directions

Pour all of the above crushed ingredients into a large empty chip bag and shake well. Enjoy!

Sweet Desserts

Samantha's Chocolate Stuffed Surprise

Contributed by: Samantha McLain

Ingredients

1 pkg. Duplex crème cookies

1 pkg. Honey bun

1 pkg. M&M's, peanut or plain (crushed)

1 pkg. Hershey bar

1 pkg. Cappuccino

Directions

Separate cookies from cream into a cup and save for icing. Crush cookies and add a little water to form dough. Separate dough in half (1/2). Layer the bottom of a bowl with the one half (1/2) of dough.

Cut the Honey bun into small pieces and place on top of dough. Melt Hershey bar and spread on top of Honey bun. Roll out the other half (1/2) of cookie dough on plastic wrap, empty chip bag etc, and then place on top of the Honey bun pieces. Now that the cake is stuffed take reserved cookie crème and cappuccino and a few tbsp. of water to make icing. Spread icing on top of cake and sprinkle with the M&M's. Enjoy!

Sweet Desserts

Commissary Critters

Contributed by: Ruben Salazar

Ingredients

1 pkg. Maria's cookies

4 pkg. Jalapeno peppers

4 pkg. cream cheese

Strawberry preserves jelly

Directions

Squeeze a ring of cream cheese on the outer rim of a Maria cookie. Drop a dab of strawberry jelly inside the ring of cream cheese and top with a slice of jalapeno pepper. Repeat until the entire pack of cookies has been prepared in this fashion. Finally pop a cookie into your mouth to experience the flavors coming together. Enjoy!

Sweet Desserts

A

Amount -a quantity of something

B

Base –the most important element or principal ingredient.

Batter –A flowing mixture of flour, milk, etc. for making pancakes.

Beef –a full-grown Ox, Cow, Bull or Steer, esp. one bred for meat.

C

Cake –a small, flat mass of baked or fried dough, batter, hashed food etc. baked as in a loaf and often covered with icing.

Camino Real Cheese –cheese that is mixed with Camino salsa comes in squeeze bottle usually sold by Cactus Anne's

Cheese –a solid food made from milk curds.

Cheesecake –a cake with cottage cheese or cream cheese.

Chicken –a common farm bird raised for its edible eggs or flesh; hen or rooster.

Chopped –to cut by blows with a sharp tool, to cut into small bits; mince: to make quick, cutting strokes; a short, sharp stroke.

Chunky –short and thick; stocky.

Cook –One who prepares food; to prepare food by boiling, baking, frying etc.; to devise or invent. Prepare, fix, warm up, warm over, stew, simmer, sear, braise, scald, broil, parch, scorch, poach, dry, chafe, fricassee, percolate, steam, bake, microwave, sauté, shirr, charbroil, griddle, brew, boil, seethe, barbeque, grill, roast, pan-fry, pan broil, deep fry, French fry, brown.

Cookie –a small, sweet cake, usually flat and either crisp or chewy.

Crust –the hard, outer part of bread; any dry hard piece of bread; the pastry shell of a pie.

D

Decorate –to adorn; ornament.

Dice –to cut vegetables, meat etc. into small cubes.

Dip –to immerse briefly, to scoop (liquid) up or out; to plunge into a liquid and quickly come out; to sink suddenly; a liquid, a sauce etc. into which something is dipped; a portion removed by dipping.

Glossary

Directions – instructions for doing, or using.

Dough – A mixture of flour, liquid, etc. worked into a soft mass for baking.

Doughy – of or like dough; soft; moldable pastry.

Drop – A bit of liquid.

F

Flour – a fine, powdery substance produced by grinding and sifting grain esp. wheat.

Fudge – a soft candy made of butter, milk, sugar, chocolate or other flavoring, etc.

G

Garnish – to decorate (food) with something that adds color or flavor.

Garlic – an herb of the lily family; it is strong smelling bulb, used as seasoning.

Granola – a breakfast cereal of rolled oats, wheat germ, sesame seeds, brown sugar or honey, diced fruits or nuts, etc.

H

Hard – firm and unyielding to the touch; solid and compact.

Haute Cuisine – the preparation of fine food by skilled chefs; food prepared in this way.

Heating element – an instrument that is used to heat water or food, etc.

Herb – any seed plant whose stem withers away annually; any plant used as medicine, seasoning, or flavoring.

Hot pot – A pot with a heating element that plugs in to the wall circuit and heats up water.

I

Icing – a mixture of variously of sugar, butter, flavoring, egg whites, etc. for covering a cake; frosting.

Ingredients – the things that a mixture is made of; components of.

Innovation – the process of introducing new methods, devices, etc.; a new method, custom, device, etc.

Instructions – any of the steps to be followed.

Immersion – the action of immersing something in a liquid

K

Knead – to work (dough) into pliable mass by folding, pressing and squeezing.

L

Layer – a single thickness, fold, etc.

M

Masa – Paste.

Mild – having a soft, pleasant flavor.

Milk – a white fluid secreted by the mammary glands of female mammals for sucking their young; cow's milk, etc. drunk by humans as a food or used to make butter, cheese, etc.

Minced – to cut up (meat etc.) into small pieces.

Mint – an aromatic plant whose leaves are used for flavoring.

Mix – to blend together in a single mass; to make by blending ingredients.

Mixture – A mixing or being mixed; something made by mixing.

Mock – sham, imitation.

Moist – slightly wet; damp.

P

Pasta – a flour paste or dough of which spaghetti, etc. is made; any food made of this.

Paste – dough for making pastry, etc.; any soft, moist, smooth preparation.

Pastry – quality of dough used for baked goods, usually flakey in texture once cooked.

Pepper, Black – a pungent condiment ground from the dried fruits of an East Indian Vine.

Peppermint – a plant of the mint family that yields pungent oil used for flavoring; the oil; a candy flavored with this oil.

Pie – a baked dish as of fruit or of meat, with an under crust or upper crust, or both.

Pizza – an Italian dish made by baking thin dough covered with tomatoes, cheese, etc.

Pkg – Package = pouch, bag.

Pork – the flesh of a pig used as food.

Portion – a helping of food.

Pot Pie – a meat pie made in deep dish.

Pot Roast – a large cut of beef cooked in one piece by braising.

Pouch – a small bag in which such meats like Chili's, Tuna, Jack Mackerels, BBQ Beef etc. are packaged and sold.

Poultry – domestic fowls, chickens, ducks etc.

Powder – any dry substance in the form of fine dust like particles, produced by crushing, grinding, etc.

Pudding – a soft sweet food make of eggs, milk, fruit, etc.

R

Ranch Dressing – creamy buttermilk salad dressing.

Recipe – a list of materials and directions for preparing a dish or drink.

S

Soak – to make thoroughly wet; to take in; absorb; moisten with liquid completely.

Salad dressing – oil, vinegar, spiced, etc. put on a salad.

Salsa – a hot sauce made with chilies, tomatoes etc.

Salt – a white, crystalline substance, sodium chloride, found in natural beds, in sea water etc., and used for seasoning food etc.; to sprinkle or season with salt; a common seasoning and preservative, table salt. Common types of flavoring slats include the following: garlic, sea, celery, onion, barbecue, salad, seasoning, hickory smoked.

Saturate – to make thoroughly soaked; to cause to be filled, charged etc. with the most if can absorb.

Sauce – a liquid or soft mixture served with food to add flavor; stewed or preserved fruit.

Sausage – port or other meat, chopped fine, seasoned, and often stuffed into a casing.

Sauté – to fry quickly with a little fat.

Scrape – to make smooth or clean by rubbing with a tool or abrasion.

Seasoning – anything that adds zest; especially salt, spices, etc. added to food.

Shake – to move quickly up and down, back and forth; to mix by brisk movements.

Shred – a narrow strip, pieces cut or torn off.

Sliced – to cut into thin sections, or pieces.

Smooth – having an even surface, with no roughness, without lumps.

Soft – giving way easily under pressure; easily cut.

Soup – a liquid food made by cooking meat, vegetables, etc. in water, milk, etc.

Soupy – loose in consistency; liquid or watery.

Sour – having the sharp, acid taste of vinegar; bitter in taste.

Spices – an aromatic vegetable substance, as nutmeg or pepper, used to season food.

Spread – a meal with many different foods; jam, butter, etc. used on bread.

Sprinkle – to scatter of all in drops, particles, or small pieces.

Squirt (sqt.) – to shoot with liquid in a jet; spurt; to wet with liquid.

Stir – to move slightly; to make active; to mix (liquid) as by agitating with a spoon.

Stir Fry – to fry (diced or sliced vegetables, meat, etc.) quickly in a wok while stirring constantly.

T

Tarts – sharp in taste, sour, acid, a small pastry shell filled with jam or jelly.

TBSP –Tablespoon

Tender – soft and easily chewed, broken or cut.

Texture – the character of food, determined by the arrangement, amount of the ingredients.

Thick – of great mass; dense.

Thorough – absolute; complete.

Tough – not easily chewed, broken or cut.

Tsp. – Teaspoon

Tube – a slender pipe of metal, glass or plastic etc. used for conveying fluids.

V

Vanilla – a plant with pod like capsules; beans. A flavoring made from these beans, used in cooking or baking; a flavoring.

W

Wafer – a thin, flat, crisp cracker or cookie.

Whip – to beat into froth.

Whisk – a kitchen utensil of wire loops used for whipping cream or mixing batter; to briskly mix together ingredients.

Wok – a bowl shaped pan used for frying.

Equivalent Package Sizes

Most recipes have the ounces of chips etc., listed, if smaller then a bag. For those recipes that say a bag here are some general bag weights. You can always add more of less to any recipe making it your own. Hot Fries 1.25 oz., Cheese Curls 2 oz., Nacho Cheese Chips 3 oz., Plain Potato Chips 3 oz., Jalapeno Chips 16 oz., Barbeque Chips 16 oz., Corn Chips 16 oz., Big Bang Chips 16 oz., Tortilla Chips 16 oz., Party Mix 16 oz., Nacho Cheese Chips 16 oz., Salsa Verde 2 oz. and Pork Skins 2 oz. Weights can change use accordingly.

Heating Sources

Throughout the recipes the cookbook mentions different types of heating sources. Heating sources are such as stingers, hot shots, hot pots, coffee pots, microwave ovens and stoves.

Many of the states department of corrections sell hot pots. Hot pots are designed to regulate water temperature. To describe a hot pot, it looks like a pitcher with a handle, a lid, a long cord to plug in and it holds about five cups of water. The heat comes from the bottom of the device much like a tea kettle on a stove. The heating element does not come in contact with the water. A popular brand sold in many states are by West Bend.

A stinger is an immersion water heater. Many of the states department of corrections sell stingers. A stinger can be described as a cord with a plug on one end and some sort of heating element on the other end. The heating element end is placed in the water, inside some sort of container like a cup, bowl, pot etc.

A hot shot is mainly like a stinger the difference being the shape and size of the heating element. These hot shots are not to be confused with hot shot water dispensers, which are one cup coffee/tea machines. Where water is poured in top area going through compartment that may contain coffee, tea or nothing and comes out of the bottom spigot hot.

The main difference between the two heating sources, stingers and hot pots are the way they heat the water. The hot pot heating element is built in and does not actually touch the water. Same goes for hot shot water dispensers. With a stinger the heating element is submerged in the water. The water is being stung or shocked which causes the water to heat.

A

APPLES

Liv's Apple Cinnamon Cheese Cake

Granola Bars

Holiday Fruity Fruit

B

BARS

Granola

Peanut Butter Fudge Bar with Peppermint Icing

Chocolate Vanilla Wafer Bars

Dream Bar Cake

BROWNIES

Charlie's Butterscotch Brownies

Rich Peanut Butter Brownies

Mock Brownies

Mud Pie Brownies

BEEF

Mexican Beef Crumble Pizza

Beef not Chop Chip Dip

Beef - n - Cheese

Jalapeno Beef Tacos

Beef Sloppy Joes

Chili and Beef Tips Pizza

Beef Enchilada

Beef Picante Soup

Texas Beef Soup

Beef Soup

BUTTERSCOTCH

Butterscotch Cream Coffee

Fudge Cookie Sandwiches w/ Butterscotch Icing

Charlies Butterscotch Brownies

C

CHICKEN

Chicken Tacos

Sharp Cheddar Chicken Nachos

Cheesy Chicken Tacos/Burritos

Chicken Salad

Chicken Soup

Chicken Noodle Tortilla Soup

Hot Buttered Soup

P.B. BBQ Chicken Dippers

Straight Strutten Chicken

Refried Beanie Chicken Weenies

Lindsey's Ritzy Pate

CHOCOLATE

Chocolatey Rich

Homemade Chocolate Cappuccino

Mississippi Mudslide

Peppermint Chocolate Milk

Chocolate Milk

Index

Loaded Caffeine Latte
Caffeine Rush
Chocolatey Peanut Butter Bars
Liv's Chocolate Cheesecake
No Bake Cookies
Wild Bill's Cream Cheese Spread
Raspberry Flavored Tootsie Pop Icing
Strawberry Vanilla Chocolate Mamas
Vanillocolate Coffee
Bananas Mores
Charlie's Butterscotch Brownies
Armadillo Eggs
White Oatmeal Cake w/ Chocolate Icing
Triple Chocolate Pie
Double Layer Chocolate Cream Pie

CHILI

Stuffed Jalapenos
Chili Spread
Todd's Tasty Tacos
Mystery Meat Tacos
Chili Pizza
Spam Pizza
Sardines Pizza
Chili Beef Tips Pizza

Chili Cheese Nachos
Diana's Stuffed Pickles
Killer Frito Pie
Sweet N Sour Noodles
Nguyen's Fried Rice
Mistie and Lacey Dip
No Meat Spread
Chicken Chili Nachos
Simple Sardines
Cumming's Sauce
Fantastic Fish Tacos
Jeff's Spaghetti Daze

CHEESE, JALAPENO SQUEEZE

Simple Sardines
Breakfast Tacos
Summer Sausage Chip Dip
Potato Salad
Commix
Spameggish Sandwich

CHEESECAKE

Banana Nut Cheesecake
Liv's Chocolate Cheesecake
Liv's Lemon Cheesecake
Liv's Apple Cinnamon Cheesecake

Strawberry Cheesecake

Ice Cream Cheesecake

D

DIPS

Mistie Lacey Dip

Summer Sausage Chip Dip

Beef-not-Chop-Chip Dip

E

EGGS

Armadillo Eggs

Bentley's Deviled Eggs

Breakfast Taco

Potato Salad

Spameggish

F

FISH – TUNA

Tuna Salad Noodle

Tuna Pizza

Fantastic Fish Tacos

Tippy's Spicy Tuna Wraps

Tuna No Soup

Diana's Stuffed Pickles

FISH - JACK MACKEREL

Spicy Mackerel Rice

Jack Mack Pizza

Lindsey's Ritzy Pate

Commix

Fantastic Fish Tacos

FISH – SARDINES

Sardines Spread

Sardines Pizza

Simple Sardines

H

HOT SAUCE / HABANERO

Chili Spread

Spicy Mackerel Rice

Todd's Tasty Tacos

Diana's Stuffed Pickles

Sweet N Sour Noodles

No Meat Spread

Hot Buttered Soup

Tuna No Soup

Fantastic Fish Tacos

Hot Salsa

I

ICING

Fudge Cookie Sandwiches w/ Butterscotch Icing

Peanut Butter Fudge Bar w/ Peppermint Icing

Nutty Chocolate Pies w/ Swirly Peanut Butter Icing

White Oatmeal Cake w/ Chocolate Icing

Index

Raspberry Flavored Tootsie Pop Icing

J

JALAPENO

- Frito Pie
- Chicken Salad
- Mexican Pizza
- Tippy's Spicy Tuna Wraps
- Fantastic Fish Tacos
- Jeff's Spaghetti Daze
- Becca's Faux Chow Chow
- Dirty's Hot Salsa

JALAPENO ZAPPOS / POTATO CHIPS

- Stuffed Jalapenos
- Spicy Mackerel Rice
- Chili/ Beef Tips Pizza
- Cheesy Chicken Burrito

K

L

M

MACKEREL

Commix

Fantastic Fish Tacos

Jack Mack Pizza

Lindsey's Ritzy Pate

Spicy Mackerel Rice

Sweet -n- Sour Bowl

N

NACHOS

- Jalapeno Cheese Nachos
- Beef N Cheese Nachos
- Chili Cheese Nachos
- Sharp Cheddar Chicken Nachos
- Chicken Chili Nachos

O

ONION POWDER / FLAKES

- Brent's Queso Loco Dip
- Lori Kay's Holiday Onion Dip
- Homemade Salsa
- Dirty's Hot Salsa
- Beef Sloppy Joe
- Jeff's Spaghetti Daze
- Lemon Fish Flips
- Mexican Pizza
- Tamales
- Fantastic Fish Tacos
- Straight Strutten Chicken

ORANGE, FRUIT
Holiday Fruity Fruit

ORANGE, JUICE
Sweet and Sour Noodles

ORANGE SPORTS DRINK
Orange Chicken

Sweet N Sour Summer Sausage

Pretty Drink

OATMEAL CRÈME PIES
Banana Nut Cheesecake

Strawberry Cheesecake

Becca's Peanut Butter Oaty Oatmeal

P

PUDDING
Diana's Banana Pudding

J.C's Lemon Pudding

Cherry's Banana Pudding

PIES
Sweet Granola Pie

Loving Lemon Meringue Pie

Sherry's Chocolate Almond Cherry Pie Delight

POWDERED, INSTANT MILK
Caffeine Latte

Caffeine Cino Rush

Allergy Sootherment

Homemade Chocolate Cappuccino

Orange Milky Mint Tea

Chocolate Milk

Simply Chocolate Milk

Peppermint Chocolate Milk

Butterscotch Cream Coffee

Vanillocolate Coffee

Health Drink

Sweet Vanilla Sin Coffee

Chocolatey Rich

Banana Nut Cheesecake

Strawberry Cheesecake

Liv's Apple Cinnamon Cheesecake

Liv's Strawberry Ice Cream Cheesecake

Liv's Chocolate Cheesecake

Loving Lemon Meringue Pie

Wild Bill's Cream Cheese Spread

Fuddy's Banana Pudding

Margaret's Creole Banana Pudding

J.C's Lemon Pudding

Sweet Granola Pie

Index

Mock Brownies
Fudge Cookie Sandwiches w/ Butterscotch Icing
Nutty Chocolate Pies w/ Peanut Butter Icing
Chocolatey Peanut Butter Bars
Chocolatey Vanilla Wafer Bars
Mickey's Peanut Butter Oatmeal
Sherry's Chocolate Almond Cherry Pie Delight
Strawberry Vanilla Chocolate Mama's
Raspberry Flavored Tootsie Pop Icing
Cookie Cereal
Cookie Dough Ice Cream

PEANUTS

Mock Brownies
Chocolate Vanilla Wafer Bars
Breakfast Bowl

PICKLE JUICE

Cruz'n Rice
Fantastic Fish Tacos
Sweet N Sour Bowl
Diana's Stuffed Pickles
Beef Sloppy Joe
Sweet N Sour Summer Sausage
Homemade Salsa
Mistie and Lacey Dip

PICKLE

Spicy Mackerel Rice
Straight Strutten Chicken
Fantastic Fish Tacos
Tippy's Spicy Tuna Wraps
Chili Beef Tips Pizza
Sweet N Sour Noodles
Wicked Popcorn Soup
Potato Salad
Diana's Stuffed Pickles

PORK SKINS

Spicy Mackerel Rice
Nguyen's Fried Rice
Sweet N Sour Chicken
Todd's Tasty Taco's
Fantastic Fish Taco's
Sweet N Sour Bowl
Diana's Stuffed Pickles
Sweet N Sour Summer Sausage

R

REFRIED BEANS, INSTANT

Refried Beanie Chicken Weenies
Todd's Tasty Tacos
Jalapeno Beef Tacos

Mystery Meat Tacos

Breakfast Tacos

Chicken Tacos

Mexican Pizza

Poor Man's Pizza

Sardines Pizza

Chili Beef Tips Pizza

Mexican Beef Crumble Pizza

Frito Pie

Chicken Chili Nachos

Sardines Spread

Slightly Sweet Nuttier Chicken

Poor Man's Spread

No Meat Spread

Potato Cake

Stuffed Jalapeno

Tuna No Soup

Chili Layer

RICE, INSTANT

Columbian Rice

Spicy Mackerel Rice

Breakfast Bowl

RANCH DRESSING

Jack Mack Pizza

Sardines Pizza

Chili Beef Tips Pizza

Commix

Tasty Spuds

Potato Cake

Lori Kay's Holiday Onion Dip

Brent's Queso Loco Dip

REGAL GRAHAM

Wild Bill's Cream Cheese Spread

S

SOUPS

Beef Flavored Soup

Chili Flavored Soup

Chicken Flavored Soup

Shrimp Flavored Soup

Picante Beef Flavored Soup

SKINS, PORK

See Pork Skins

SWEETENER

Spicy Mackerel Rice

Fantastic Fish Tacos

Sweet N Sour Bowl

Diana's Stuffed Pickles

Breakfast Tacos

Index

Pretty Drink

Sweet Orange Mint Tea

Caffeine Latte

Caffeine Cino Rush

Homemade Chocolate Cappuccino

Orange Milky Mint Tea

Chocolate Milk

Green Hulk Cold Drink

Remember Bennigans

SALAD DRESSING

Simply Scrumptious Ham Mac N Cheese

Potato Salad

Tuna Noodle Salad

Tuna No Soup

Bentley's Deviled Eggs

Special Sauce

A La Sauce

Homemade Sandwich Spread

Brent's Queso Loco Dip

SANDWICH SPREAD

Spameggish Sandwich

Sweet N Sour Bowl

SOY SAUCE

Columbian Rice

SALSA

Chicken Noodle Tortilla Soup

Straight Strutten Chicken

Todd's Tasty Tacos

Mystery Meat Tacos

Breakfast Tacos

No Meat Spread

Tuna No Soup

Beef–not–Chop-Chip Dip

Summer Sausage Chip Dip

SPRITE

Liv's Lemon Cheesecake

Liv's Apple Cinnamon Cheesecake

Liv's Strawberry Ice Cream Cheesecake

Liv's Chocolate Cheesecake

J.C's Lemon Pudding

SNICKERS

Strawberry Cheesecake

Snickers Cake

Luscious Lava Nut Cake

Sherry's Chocolate Almond Cherry Pie Delight

T

TUNA

Fantastic Fish Tacos

Tippy's Spicy Tuna Wraps

Tuna Pizza

TORTILLA, FLOUR

    Straight Strutten Chicken

    Todd's Tasty Tacos

    Jalapeno Beef Tacos

    Mystery Meat Tacos

    Tacos a La TDCJ

    Breakfast Tacos

    Chicken Tacos

    Fantastic Fish Tacos

    Tippy's Spicy Tuna

    Cheesy Chicken Burrito

    Chipotle Chicken and Ranch Burrito

    Spicy Chicken Burrito

    Sweet N Sour Noodles

    Commix

    Chili Layer

THREE MUSKETEERS

    Liv's Chocolate Cheesecake

    Extra Sweet Honey Bun

U

V

VANILLA CRÈME COOKIES

    Ice Cream Cheesecake

    Liv's Lemon Cheesecake

    Liv's Apple Cinnamon Cheesecake

    Liv's Strawberry Ice Cream Cheesecake

    Loving Lemon Meringue Pie

    Sweet Granola Pie

    Fudge Cookie Sandwiches w/ Butterscotch Icing

    Peanut Butter Fudge Bar w/ Peppermint Icing

    Nutty Chocolate Pies w/ Peanut Butter Icing

    Chocolatey Peanut Butter Bars

    Dream Bar Cake

    Snickers Cake

    Luscious Lava Nut Cake

    Sherry's Chocolate Almond Cherry Pie Delight

    Tippy's Coffee Balls

W

WAFER, VANILLA

    Fruddy's Banana Pudding

    Margaret's Creole Banana Pudding

    Cherry's Banana Pudding

    Diana's Banana Pudding

    J.C's Lemon Pudding

    Charlie's Butterscotch Brownies

    Chocolate Vanilla Wafer Bars

    Armadillo Eggs

About the Author

The author is a native of Texas, currently 28 year old and single with no children. He enjoys cooking, baking, reading, writing and keeping busy. He has hopes of one day of making something of himself and starting a family.

NEW BOOK-ALL DIFFERENT RECIPES

NEW 2nd Edition

The CELL CHEF

NEW 2nd Edition

To order a copy of...

The CELL CHEF Cookbook II

Only $13.99 Plus $5 S/H with tracking

Softcover, Square 8.25" x 8.25", 180+ pages
NO ORDER FORM NEEDED clearly write on paper & send payment to:
Freebird Publishers, Box 541, North Dighton, MA 02764
Online at FreebirdPublishers.com, Amazon.com and B&N.com
Toll Free: 888-712-1987   Text/Phone: 774-406-8682

For more information send two stamps.

NEW BOOKS BEING PUBLISHED EVERY MONTH

FREEBIRD PUBLISHERS

SPECIALIZING IN PRISONER PUBLICATIONS

BOX 541, N. DIGHTON, MA 02764

FREEBIRDPUBLISHERS.COM

WE NEED YOUR REVIEWS

Rate Us & Win!

We do monthly drawings for a FREE copy of one of our publications. Just have your loved one rate any Freebird Publishers book on Amazon and then send us a quick e-mail with your name, inmate number, and institution address and you could win a FREE book.

FREEBIRD PUBLISHERS
Box 541
North Dighton, MA 02764

www.freebirdpublishers.com
Diane@FreebirdPublishers.com

FREEBIRD PUBLISHERS

Thanks for your interest in Freebird Publishers!

We value our customers and would love to hear from you! Reviews are an important part in bringing you quality publications. We love hearing from our readers-rather it's good or bad (though we strive for the best)!

If you could take the time to review/rate any publication you've purchased with Freebird Publishers we would appreciate it!

If your loved one uses Amazon, have them post your review on the books you've read. This will help us tremendously, in providing future publications that are even more useful to our readers and growing our business.

Amazon works off of a 5 star rating system. When having your loved one rate us be sure to give them your chosen star number as well as a written review. Though written reviews aren't required, we truly appreciate hearing from you.

Sample Review Received on Inmate Shopper

☆☆☆☆☆ **Everything a prisoner needs is available in this book.**
June 7, 2018
Format: Paperback

A necessary reference book for anyone in prison today. This book has everything an inmate needs to keep in touch with the outside world on their own from inside their prison cell. Inmate Shopper's business directory provides complete contact information on hundreds of resources for inmate services and rates the companies listed too! The book has even more to offer, contains numerous sections that have everything from educational, criminal justice, reentry, LGBT, entertainment, sports schedules and more. The best thing is each issue has all new content and updates to keep the inmate informed on todays changes. We recommend everybody that knows anyone in prison to send them a copy, they will thank you.

Made in the USA
Middletown, DE
14 October 2024